FINDING PEAKS AND VALLEYS IN A FLAT WORLD
GOODNESS, TRUTH, AND MEANING IN THE MIDST OF TODAY'S MAD CHASE FOR PROSPERITY AND INSTANT FEEDBACK

Mark Ellingsen

Interdenominational Theological Center

Series in Philosophy of Religion

VERNON PRESS

www.vernonpress.com

In the Americas:	*In the rest of the world:*
Vernon Press	Vernon Press
1000 N West Street, Suite 1200	C/Sancti Espiritu 17,
Wilmington, Delaware, 19801	Malaga, 29006
United States	Spain

Series in Philosophy of Religion

Library of Congress Control Number: 2020947142

ISBN: 978-1-64889-245-5

Also available: 978-1-64889-108-3 [Hardback]; 978-1-64889-156-4 [PDF, E-Book]

Cover design by Vernon Press using elements designed by Freepik and Free-Photos from Pixabay.

TABLE OF CONTENTS

ACKNOWLEDGMENTS   vii

FOREWORD   ix
Will Willimon
Duke Divinity School

INTRODUCTION WHAT MAKES THE WORLD FLAT?   xi

Chapter 1   PROBLEMS IN A FLAT WORLD   1

Chapter 2   EVERYDAY LIFE IN A FLAT WORLD   11

Chapter 3   REMEDY TO OUR DESPAIR: INTRODUCTION TO THE PHILOSOPHY OF SOREN KIERKEGAARD   21

Chapter 4   AESTHETIC LIFE: DESCENDING INTO THE FLAT WORLD'S VALLEYS   29

Chapter 5   ETHICAL LIFE: CONSTRUCTING SOME PEAKS AND FINDING SOME JUSTICE IN A FLAT WORLD   39

Chapter 6   RELIGIOUS LIFE: FROM THE SHALLOWS TO THE MOUNTAIN-TOP   51

CONCLUSION   61

BIBLIOGRAPHY   69

INDEX   73

FOR

DAVE

STEVE AND LYNN

For more than half of century of friendship, fun, games, and
good conversation

ACKNOWLEDGMENTS

If life in our globalized economy and interconnected world is as challenging as it seems to be for a lot of us, as difficult as I seem to say it is in this book, I must confess that I haven't found life in our context so impossible and completely unsatisfying. Of course, the author of a book aiming to help you cope had better be pretty competent in executing the advice he gives, to have found what he advises to be personally helpful. It is true that I've been trying to take the great 19th-century Philosopher Søren Kierkegaard's advice on how to cope, trying to leap away from aestheticism, too much dour morality, and trying to become a Christian and have fun doing it. That will be my (Kierkegaardian) advice to you in this book. But along the way, I've had some advantages that a lot of us daring to live that way don't have. I'm not really the "solitary individual" in these quests. I've had a number of precious friends. I think first of my wife of 48 years Betsey, who does a lot of editing of my books. But then I've had two friends, Dave Lawton and Steve Strumlok who've known me more than half a century (back to elementary school in Dave's case and since freshman year of college in the case of Steve). Soccer teammates in high school and college ball respectively. And I've known Steve's special wife Lynn almost as long as I have known Betsey. All of us are teachers in some way (I'm the odd man out, not working in public schools like all of them.) We've maintained these friendships, though separated by thousands of miles sometimes (even without internet connectivity). Had he not died tragically in his 20s serving his country in the military, our dear friend Pat Smith would have been included in this number too, and he's not forgotten whenever we get together. With special lifetime friends like I have, life gets a lot easier, and this book will tell you a little bit why.

What's really neat about dedicating this book to my longest-term friends is that even before Betsey and Lynn and Dave's special ladies came into the picture, Steve and Dave and I encountered Kierkegaard, and back in our 20s were already thinking together about what he might have to say to us about life. How appropriate, then, that this book is for them, and Betsey who's already had 9 of these book dedications from me thought so too. I might not have felt ready to tell you about Kierkegaard had I not had all these years talking about him with these friends. So thanks, life-long friends, for all the support, the good times, and the feeling that you and I have got each other's backs through thick and thin, even when the world feels flat.

FOREWORD

Will Willimon
Duke Divinity School

I've just gotten around to reading David Epstein's *Range: Why Generalists Triumph in a Specialized World.* The complex, wicked problems that we face require generalized thinking and an ability to make connections with seemingly disparate fields of knowledge. As a pastor, a preacher—that is, as a generalist par excellence—I found encouragement in Epstein's praise of conversation between academic disciplines.

Mark Ellingsen's *Peaks and Valleys in a Flat World* is a remarkable exercise in creative connection-making in service to more abundant living in today's world. Mark successfully performs the seemingly unlikely feat of introducing cultural commentator Thomas Friedman to Nineteenth-Century theologian/philosopher Søren Kierkegaard. The collaborative conversation that emerges is remarkable.

After analyzing the nature of contemporary life in the technologically flattened world with its insane pursuit of material prosperity and lust for instant gratification, Ellingsen asks Kierkegaard to speak to our modern quandary. Using SK's typology of the aesthetic, the ethical, and the religious modes of existence, Ellingsen discovers fresh insights that startle us with sparkling insights and immediate applicability.

Throughout my own life, at certain key moments, Kierkegaard—that allegedly "melancholy Dane"—has brought me joy by giving me just the word that I needed to hear, just the right handle to grab hold of perplexing reality, whether I wanted to hear his truth or not. I'm sure that under Ellingsen's lively, skilled reading of SK, he will do the same for you.

Noble words like "truth," "goodness," and "meaning" are brushed off and used to challenge a culture in which many of us seem to have gained the whole world but lost our souls. Ellingsen's is a remarkable achievement: to give us a trenchant critique of contemporary life combined with a hopeful, practical way through the peaks and valleys.

Will Willimon

Professor of the Practice of Christian Ministry, Duke Divinity School, author of *Accidental Preacher: A Memoir.*

INTRODUCTION
WHAT MAKES THE WORLD FLAT?

"The World Is Flat!" The title of Thomas Friedman's best-seller has almost become a mantra for our time. But what is life like for those of us living in our new globalized economic order? It's so bewildering, so draining, so uncertain, and even so lonely sometimes. This is a book about how to thrive in our new contexts, and if you're a Christian, it's also a book about how to live faithfully in the flat world.

In some ways, things are better. Globalization has fostered international competition, to the benefit of the consumer. Combined with the computer revolution, it has provided a leveled playing field making it possible for smaller companies to compete with the large international corporations and also individual empowerment. The start-up company has marketing resources and the ability to do research, in some cases even means of production, comparable to the mega-corporation. And the individual is likewise empowered in ways unthinkable before the 1990s. We have a global communications platform and can conduct research at an astronomical speed. Collaboration and individualization which allows us to create our own values are now the order of the day. All of us can now become celebrities – at least on YouTube.

Because these new opportunities are, in principle available to anyone with the skills to compete, regardless of social standing or the old company hierarchy, the old hierarchies which gave some insuperable advantage are abolished. Class distinctions have been flattened. And because these new possibilities extend all over the world, Friedman concluded that the world is flat.

Friedman proceeds to describe some of the characteristics of the flat word which make these other developments and opportunities possible. The world is flat, he maintains, insofar as we live in a business environment in which low –cost interconnectivity and global networks for collaboration, providing business owners all over the world the ability to pull together low-cost labor and high levels of technology have reached hitherto unimaginable levels.[1]

As we are all well aware, though, there have been costs for these technological developments and the new opportunities they have created. At least we can speak of new challenges we now face as a result.

With the new individual opportunities has come an eroding sense of tradition and community. In a business environment in which flexibility, adaptability, creativity, a willingness to change, and team-work on short-term teams are keys to success, there is less and less need for tradition or institutional memory. On the job, you learn to eye with suspicion long-standing traditions and communities which have endured for generations. Besides, workers cannot count on being at a job for decades since lifetime employment with a company is no longer a way of life in the flat world. These dynamics may not immediately translate into a total rejection of community and tradition, but at least your subliminal bias is to retreat from these investments.

Likewise, even the teamwork, the collaborative style of successful businesses in the flat world undermines traditional values and a sense of community. The teams and the collaboration undertaken for the sake of growing the market or establishing the supply chain are not created for the sake of establishing long-term relationships. They are formed for short-term tasks, or at least until the next stage of the business cycle renders them obsolete. Because you are not likely to remain in touch with your colleagues and co-workers your entire working life, indeed in the flexible economy you probably will not stay with the company for your whole career, you are actually alone at work, just working for yourself along with others. The long-term friendships among co-workers that used to develop when lifetime jobs were the norm are not likely to form in the flat world. And this may subliminally create a sense of distance from one's own political community, if not one's family.

It may be that it takes "people-skills" in the flat world in view of the networking and teamwork that have become a way of life in modern business. But these dynamics tend to create a superficiality in relationships. In a therapeutically dominated ethos like ours (all the major businesses contract or hold retreats with psychologists), conflict is perceived as bad for business (just as American society as a whole has come to look askance at conflict and debate). This encourages masking ill feelings, being a people person who is always hiding one's real self. In addition, you have to be cautious in your relationships, because colleagues on your team are ultimately competitors. Thus I had better not share my true self and all my skills, or they could be used against me by these colleagues. If I share all I know, I am no longer indispensable.

This sense of distance creates a sense of irony about life. Because of the need to be flexible and a people-oriented team player, but never with the full investment of one's self, the flat world effectively nurtures workers who are ironic. The ironic character type is Narcissistic. Such people are willing to compromise what they stand for in order to advance their careers. They stand for nothing; they are empty.

Later in the book, I will explore with you how and why this style of life leads to unhappiness. Together we will consider cutting-edge research on the human brain which demonstrates why such a life leads to unhappiness. The first two chapters also address this matter.

The Neurobiological research we'll consider also provides clues regarding how we can find happiness in the flat world. These insights converge, interestingly enough, with the thought of the great 19th-century Christian philosopher, Søren Kierkegaard. This Danish writer is often identified as the founder of or inspiration for Existentialist philosophy. Kierkegaard hypothesizes that one cannot find fulfillment in life without experiencing fear or sickness of the soul. We need valleys if we are to find mountain-top experiences. This is what I mean by peaks and valleys in the flat world Chapter Three explores Kierkegaard's thinking, especially about three stages of human existence. He believed that most people live aesthetically, that is, as works of art, trying to find what is beautiful and enjoyable to them. This is a feel-good mode of existence that makes no commitments. Such people are ironic in the sense of never defining themselves by taking a stand. They are eminently adaptable to circumstances, seeking enjoyment in order to avoid boredom. But a combination of this analysis with a close look at life in a flat world reveals that this is the way most Americans live. We'll explore this point in the fourth chapter along with some of the recent research on the human brain I just mentioned. The analysis will help us understand the why of what we already know – that the flexible, self-concerned lifestyle we need to succeed (or cope) in the flat world does not lead to happiness. In fact, it results in a life of despair.

Though Kierkegaard was a Christian who believed that we can only have a meaningful life if we live in faith, he did not think that the way to move people to such faith was to preach to those living aesthetically. Such individuals, he correctly postulated, will not hear the Gospel. If they attend church it is only because it feels good to them – is entertaining or meets their needs. In order to get a hearing for faith, Kierkegaard and I are concerned to provide another alternative for living in the flat world, a way of life in which people will have a little more to live for, one which is more conducive to appreciating the religious way of life as a viable option in the flat world.

In Chapter Five, this Ethical way of life and what it might look like in a flat world receives attention. Again Kierkegaard's analysis is most helpful. In his view, Ethical people have leaped to this mode of existence after realizing that the aesthetic life of the successful denizens of the flat world leads to despair. In that valley, they yearn for a mountaintop, a place above the hustle and bustle and meaninglessness of the rat race. They find these mountaintops in living lives dedicated to high ideals.

According to Kierkegaard, people committed to an Ethical mode of existence are not spectators, like Aesthetic people who flexibly go with the flow. They are individuals who make free decisions which define who they are. For this reason, they experience a more intense self-concern.

We'll explore in this chapter what an Ethical way of life might look like in a flat world. Some of Friedman's suggestions are on target in sketching such a lifestyle, but he is inadequate in helping us to thrive. I will propose ways, already working well in several Scandinavian nations, to remain compassionate in a flat world.

Ultimately, though, Kierkegaard makes clear, that even the Ethical mode of existence fails to deliver goodness, truth, and meaning. As we'll observe in Chapter Five, an ethical lifestyle drops us into a valley from its promised peak. Kierkegaard helps us to recognize that ethical people eventually come to despair over living a morally perfect life. Even apparent saints fall short of their ideals. We never can fully reconcile what is to what should be. Kierkegaard calls such despair the "sickness unto death."[3] Religious life becomes an attractive alternative to such people, a way of coping with despair. Only ethical people are really able to hear the Word of God, to be raised to the peaks even in a flat world.

The remainder of the book explores these themes, what Kierkegaard calls the Religious way of life. He envisions religious life as a paradoxical style of existence, one that isn't reasonable in the strongest sense of the word. In fact it is a lifestyle that, while outwardly engaging the ways of the world, actually contradicts the world's values and operates at cross-purposes with the world. We'll see that this vision entails a life that, while recognizing that the world is flat and that you have to practice some flexibility in order to cope, religious life needs to be lived on the edge – so consumed with God that the things of the world ultimately do not matter while still living among them. The religious life is a life lived on a mountaintop, while ever on the edge of the fragility of life (of the valleys) in a flat world. People trying to become Christian in a flat world are so single-mindedly and passionately devoted to eternal realities that these convictions outweigh all the demands for flexibility and creative sensitivity to one's environs. Such people truly stand for something; they are saturated by a relationship in passion which renders all that they do and think to be of eternal significance.

Of course, Kierkegaard also makes clear that this mode of existence involves renunciation, even suffering. Because human life (life in the flat world) is an illness, to align oneself with the joys of eternity is to put oneself in tension, to suffer. One suffers when going against the grain of what seems reasonable in the flat world. But we will see that this lifestyle provides significant resources for living in this world of ours. The individual trying to become a Christian is in the process of becoming.[4] In that sense, such a person is open, even to a point flexible. We will see in more detail how this is a mode of existence that can offer meaning, joy, and fulfillment in a flat world.

There are exciting neurobiological research results which seem to authorize these conclusions about the validity of applying Kierkegaardian advice to the flat world. It seems that when human beings are preoccupied with themselves and their circumstances the back parts of their brain (the parietal lobe) are activated. This segment of the brain orients us in space and time. But it is only when the front part of the brain (esp. the frontal lobe) is activated that pleasurable neurochemicals which promote pleasure and health are secreted and flow in the brain. This part of the brain which is saturated by these chemicals (the executive part of the brain) is activated especially when we become less focused on ourselves (when we renounce/ aesthetic modes of existence) in favor of projects bigger than we are. In other words, the Ethical mode and even more so, the Religious mode of existence are more likely to offer joy and fulfillment than a life dedicated only to success in the flat world.

With this background, the Conclusion provides some advice on how to live religiously in the flat world. You will have the opportunity to explore some ways that you can use Kierkegaard's insights to help you find some peaks and valleys. You'll learn some ways to break free of meaningless reinvention of yourself, be reminded of the sense of meaning ethical conviction can offer (and the sorts of moral commitments that are especially pressing in our flat world), along with spiritual exercises which can aid you to recognize that even this morality ultimately leads to emptiness, that only a leap of faith into the loving arms of God can break off the monotonous meaninglessness of life in the flat world.

Our map for exploring the ups and downs of life lies before you. But first, we need to clarify for ourselves what it's really like to live in this flat world that today's economic forces have created.

NOTES

1. Thomas L. Friedman, The World Is Flat: A Brief History of the Twenty-First Century (paperback ed.; New York: Pacidor/Farrar, Straus and Giroux, 2007), esp. pp.400,8,449-457.
2. For these insights, I have learned from Richard Sennett, The Corrosion of Character: The Personal Consequences of Work in the New Capitalism (New York and London: W. W. Norton & Company, 1998), esp. pp.23-25.
3. Søren Kierkegaard, The Sickness Unto Death (Copenhagen, 1849).
4. Søren Kierkegaard, Concluding Unscientific Postscript, trans. David F. Swenson and Walter Lowrie (Princeton,NJ: Princeton University Press, 1941), pp.403-406.

Chapter 1

PROBLEMS IN A FLAT WORLD

We've already noted how *New York Times* columnist Thomas Friedman proclaimed that the world is flat. He was referring to the phenomenon of *Globalization*. Since the Computer Revolution, if not as long as the Industrial Revolution of the 1800s (it really began with Columbus and the discovery of America), different parts of the world have been increasingly connected in the expansion of international cultural, economic, and political activities. Globalization is all about developing trade practices, means of communication, and changing cultural patterns to facilitate these connections.[1] Let's flesh out how globalization manifests itself, so we can understand what it is doing to us, what life is like for most of us in a world that knows no or few boundaries.

Friedman maintains that globalization has been shaped by a triple convergence. The new computer technology created a global platform enabling individuals, groups, companies, and universities all over the world to collaborate. Geography, distance, time, and culture no longer prevent collaboration. This convergence has made possible the inclusion of new players in the economic game, persons and institutions from regions beyond Western capitalism (like Russia, China, Eastern Europe, Central and South America, as well as Africa). The third convergence was the new style of management, which more and more characterizes businesses well before the computer revolution. Since late in the 20th-century management techniques began to move away from a vertical chain of command to a more horizontal style of management.[2]

This administrative shift was a function of the gradual post-1960s realization that short-term profits are preferable to long-term stability. The market is consumer-driven mandating that we can never do business the same way year to year. The implication of this for management practice is to favor loose networks which are more open to decisive reinvention than are pyramidal hierarchies. This has led to stress on teams and teamwork to deal with short-term tasks. Leaders and so businesses as a whole need to be able to let go of the past and accept fragmentation.[3] As noted in the introduction, the result is that experience does not matter as much, and loyalty to employees is diminished, for if you are too loyal to your employees, you and your business may not be flexible enough to meet the latest realities of the market. The most successful managers or employees in the corporation are those who can be flexible (ready to take on new jobs, readily relocate residences and hours, and also not be committed to perduring strategies or values). This may easily translate into stress on "people skills" and "networking" over accomplishment.

Another dynamic of this approach to management is that the stress on teamwork discourages debate and adversary relationships between labor and management in the interests of the "team." Once the worker can no longer operate in a climate that he/she has the power to confront the boss, then the manager can more readily dismiss the disgruntled worker/s/ as a troublemaker. On teams, you are all supposed to pull together, and so although the myth of team management is that workers have more authority in the company as they now share authority with the boss, in fact, workers now find themselves in a less welcoming atmosphere in which to challenge lower wages and more hours worked, lest they be deemed disruptive to the team.

The need for flexibility and a climate in which you had better not say what you really think if it does not accord with the team's consensus (it's usually all about what the boss wants without his/her saying it) has implications for everyday lifestyle. More of that in the next chapter.

Before we begin to consider what personal and interpersonal challenges globalization poses, let's review its institutional manifestations in more detail first.

WHAT GLOBALIZATION LOOKS LIKE

The analyst who first spoke of globalization as flattening the world, Thomas Friedman, offers us a helpful analysis of the characteristics of globalization (he speaks of "flatteners.")[4] It is quite evident in internet connectivity enabling collaboration among those all over the globe. As a result, small businesses can be just as profitable and influential as big businesses, for their advertising outreach can be comparable. Communities gain more power, since they no longer need "middle-men" (third parties) to approve their work or assist them in order for those insights to become influential. Likewise, individuals are now empowered, because they are not just consumers, but with unlimited access to electronic means of growing the market can more readily become successful producers of goods and services. Youtube and the ability to publish books on the internet are just two of the numerous examples that could be cited to illustrate this flattener. The development of Microsoft and Facebook or Google are obvious examples.

Globalization would not be fully implemented if corporations did not engage in outsourcing their work and even offshoring it. In a globalized business context, with fierce competition and ever-changing dynamics, you can only compete if your production costs are way down, and that will not happen if you limit your labor pool to nations with a limited number of workers who will demand higher wages and lots of concessions. Besides, when you include in your labor force workers from other communities/nations, you tend to grow your market as well and get around trade barriers which might be imposed in the nations of your labor force on foreign goods and services. The implications of these dynamics for the American labor force are akin to what has happened as a result of the new styles of team management. More of that later.

Another factor in our globalized economy is efficient, international supply-chaining. Walmart is probably the poster-child for this practice. Of course, a supply chain is a network between a company and its suppliers in order to produce and distribute a specific product to the final buyer. This network includes different activities, people, entities, information, and resources. The supply chain also represents the steps it takes to get the product or service from its original state to the customer. Of course, the aim is to have the lowest costs possible and a fast production cycle, so that good profits can still be made on what is sold while keeping the price lower than one's competitors. Wal-Mart has perfected this by finding low-cost manufacturers and producers of its products/foods. Then the company perfected its supply chain throughout the world from those producing the products to its distribution centers. The detailed comprehensive data it amasses on what its customers buy is transmitted to all manufacturers in the chain ensuring that the shelves are always stocked with just the right items at the right time. These cost-saving measures entail the ability to sell goods at the lowest competitive prices and lots of efficiency.

Note that information is a big part of the efficient supply chain. Gaining information about the customer is crucial. Of course, search engines like Google as well as Facebook regularly accumulate that sort of data about what our preferences and interests are. It is all essential input for a business in a globalized world. (Note the connections here between this personal data and the supply chain procedures of the Walmarts and also how essential the gathering of such personal information is sensitive to changes in the market which all successful companies must exhibit today.)

There's a cost to the consumer and the worker in these changes. Privacy is increasingly under siege.[5] Of course, the average American leading a law-abiding life might not mind. But suppose some youthful indiscretion becomes public when you are seeking that new job? Even if such privacy concerns don't trouble you, let's consider some other implications of the flat world which might be of concern. At least they remind us that life has changed in the flat world. More individuals than ever before have the power to create their own content and globalize it. But is this freedom to create and even to become a "known commodity" all over the world worth the trade-offs we now explore?

THINGS AIN'T THE SAME ANYMORE: CHALLENGES IN THE FLAT WORLD

The outsourcing and offshoring of jobs entailed for successful businesses in the flat world and its globalized economy involves a loosening of the links between companies and their host nations. In these contexts, what is good for Ford or for Microsoft and Walmart, is not necessarily good for the American worker. These loosening ties explain why globalization has not been good for a lot of people who enjoyed better times in the old economic system.[6] And as we'll note in the next chapter, these dynamics do nothing to enhance the loyalty of American workers to their companies, and even effectively undermines national loyalty (patriotism). What is good for me economically may be in tension with my nation, and so I ultimately owe loyalty to myself and my own interests.

With this loosening of business' loyalty to its workforce an ethos is created in which it is good business to eliminate extraneous positions and to keep labor expenses to a minimum. Even proponents of globalization concede the realities of today, speaking of short-term job losses.[7]

If you have investments in these businesses, or have an untouchable job in one of them (have the education or skills to make you irreplaceable), times are good. But given the lower salaries for those at the bottom or in the middle of the economy, globalization has widened the rich-poor gap. The U.S. Census Bureau reported that in 2018 American households in the top fifth of earners brought in 52% of the U.S. income, more than the lower 4/5s of the economy. The income gap is greater in the U.S. than in any of the other G-7 nations. In 1968, by comparison, the top-earning 20% of households brought in 43% of the nation's income, while those in the lower four income quintiles accounted for 56%. Among the top 5% of households – those with incomes of at least $248,729 in 2018 – their share of all U.S. income rose from 16% in 1968 to 23% in 2018.[8]

Of course, we love those cheaper prices that all the outsourcing and offshoring the Walmarts and the foreign cars can provide. But how about the stagnant wages for most of us, the fact that many of Walmarts' employees are poor enough to qualify for Medicaid?[9] But as globalization champion Thomas Friedman concedes, "... the flattening of the world is going to be hugely disruptive to both traditional and developed societies. The weak will fall further behind faster." This is an era of creative destruction, he adds.[10]

True enough, with larger networks with which we have to engage (for the whole world is both a market but also companies and peers in virtually every nation are also our competitors) there must be an emphasis on teamwork and collaboration.[11] But in fact we are much more on our own. Job security in a business ethos dedicated to outsourcing, flexibility, and responsiveness to the immediate needs of the market is a thing of the past. The average Millennial worker will not spend a career with just 1 or 2 companies. And then there is the reality in a globalized ethos that you have more competitors, entailing that more demands are placed on the business and its labor force.[12] No wonder Americans have not worked as hard as they have in the last decade since the days of the pre-Labor Union sweatshops. We'll discuss the implications of this kind of individualism and nose-to-the-grindstone lifestyle in the next chapter.

For all the connections made in the globalized ethos, the need for (artificial) collaboration, ultimately one is all alone in "making it." Success is up to me and me alone. Even friends of the globalization process concede that technology can alienate us from those nearest to us.[13] Life on the internet is scattered. You can be doing a lot of things simultaneously (view the screen, glance at the TV, talk to someone else in the room, or just daydream). And Neurobiologists have observed that something insalubrious may happen to our brains with widespread and persistent use of the internet.

It seems that this sort of scattered way of life entails less use of the part of our brain which truly makes us human, the prefrontal cortex. This is the administrative portion of our brains, responsible for controlling our emotions and especially active in cooperative efforts. It is not as active when we are not concentrating. This (front) part of the brain is also essential to assessing new information based on past memory, as neurons in that part of the brain must facilitate connections with neurons in other parts of the brain in order for the present memory to become long-term. And if you do not make new brain connections, you do not think new thoughts, have creative insights. Since the human brain operates with the principle "use it or lost it," if you de-activate the frontal cortex of your brain long enough by engaging most of the time in scattered activities, your ability to retain information and think creatively will be lost.[14] Heavy internet use undermines the depth of our thought, shallows our thinking, turns us inward on ourselves. For all the advantages the internet provides the globalized ethos it may be undermining the very characteristics we need in order to thrive and succeed in a flat world.

A preoccupation with the self (since we are all celebrities on the Internet and are responsible to no one but ourselves if we are to succeed in a globalized ethos) nurtures a kind of Narcissism, a preoccupation with the agendas of the self and self-fulfillment such that everyone and everything becomes nothing more than a vehicle for making the self feel good .[15] This helps account for how the older segments of the Millennial Generation, native to the internet, poll as increasingly Narcissistic.[16] Of course, it should be noted that Narcissism levels have lessened among younger Millennials (the so-called iGens born since the 1980s) who have only known internet life. But in their case, Narcissism seems to have been replaced in their case by disengagement and cynicism.[17] Even more seriously is internet addiction, which is related to our inability to focus on the "now" of our interpersonal interactions, to put the "likes" of Facebook or the New Mail and incoming calls on the cellphone ahead of the immediate needs of spouse, friends, or children.[18]

There are some significant challenges to be faced by Americans and all denizens in our flat world. More on that in the next chapter. But there is another challenge which globalization poses to culture and nations that we need to consider. It has implications for personal well-being as well.

The most violent, passionate reactions against globalization, evident in Muslim terrorism, Brexit, as well as other expressions of the new European and American Nationalism testify to challenges the new world reality raises for ordinary men and women worldwide (but especially those not located in the new centers of power). There is a feeling in these circles that those with power over the globalized mechanisms (Western nations in general, the rich, and whites in America) are using these economic dynamics and social media to impose their agenda and values on minority communities and on less-developed nations and their cultures – to Westernize or "whitenize" everyone. Proponents of globalization like Thomas Friedman may object on grounds of the empowering character of globalizing, contending that it offers giving an international market to the small entrepreneur and the developing nation, allowing those who desire to remain in their homeland without having to emigrate to the West to get the good jobs.[19]

Let's grant Friedman's argument. But even if we do, we cannot deny the ill feelings and perceptions of the poor and marginalized, in the West and in developing nations. They have a point. Korea and Japan, as well as Norway, is a lot more "American" than they were at the beginning of the 20th century. Africa is a lot more "Westernized" than prior to Colonialism. A 2018 poll conducted by the Pew Research Center found that 67% of South Koreans, 64% of Mexicans, 57% of Argentinians, 53% of Brazilians, and nearly half the populations of Germany, France, Indonesia, and Kenya found U.S power and influence to be a major threat to their nations. An earlier Washington Post-ABC news poll in 2011 found that 70% of women, 73% of African Americans, and 66% of all citizens in the Fly-Over Midwestern States believe that globalization has been bad for American jobs. These polls not only reflect geographical biases of the locations of the cutting-edge businesses of the globalized world, but also the fact that white men tend to dominate in the leadership of these businesses and in Computer Science majors in the elite universities.[20]

These realities cannot be denied. And even the proponents of globalization concede that globalization will cause job displacement (some jobs will inevitably be off-shored or eliminated) and also exacerbate some of the existing economic disparities (like racism and sexism). The poor will inevitably be most affected by these developments.[21]

Cheerleader for globalization Thomas Friedman notes yet one more dynamic and unintended consequence of the rush towards globalization. He has observed a sense of entitlement among today's Americans, less ambition. This may be a function of the fast-moving economy associated with globalization. It has nurtured a focus on consumption, because in an ever-changing economy short-term profits over long-term investment are the priority for business executives. American life is all about "spending" After all, George Bush's first words after the catastrophe of 9/11 was to urge Americans to "go shopping for their families." Friedman notes that this sense of entitlement is not just a function of this ethos which prioritizes consumption over hard work, of immediate gratification over long-term thinking, but is also related to the lowering of educational standards.[22] According to a 2017 study of the Programme for International Student Assessment the US ranks 13th in reading among the nations and according to a 2018 study of the program ranks 26th among the nations in Math, behind Japan, China, Germany, most of the other Western European nations. The National Survey of Student Engagement found in 2014 that college students just spent 17 hours studying per week! (The norm for a full-time student has been 45 hours per week.) You don't get much hard work out of people who feel entitled. Add to these dynamics how the Narcissism and stress on relational skills which are cultivated by the Team-Management business dynamics of globalization and life on the net further erode the work ethic.

It seems that the team concept makes it harder to judge excellence in one's job, in comparison to the older management paradigm when individual accountability for a specific assignment is the model. Consequently, promotions and dismissals tend not to be based on clear, fixed rules, with crisply defined tasks. How one relates to networks has become the determining factor in measuring one's professional success.[23] The lack of clarity about these standards creates either anxiety, for in the old system you knew where you stood. It can also undermine a work ethic. The measure for success in this vacuum either becomes public recognition, and in some cases, that feeds the new materialism and acquisitions-mania we've noted. We're led to mad consumption in order to get the public recognition we crave, since what we do does not offer an objective standard of our worth.

The Team Management style associated with doing business in a globalized ethos also contributes to shaping the personalities of managers and labor force. The good team player must be flexible, for the team's decision cannot be bucked, even if you disagree. In fact, the boss needs to give the impression of just being part of the team, even while he or she is manipulating all the team members. The company man/woman has no ownership of his or her actions or thoughts, for what I actually do in such an ethos is play to the crowd, give the audience what it wants. As we've already noted, such a member of the labor force inevitably becomes ironic, sensing that nothing ultimately matters in what I do except how the boss and those I supervise perceive me. Emptied as I am by such performances for the sake of my career, for what I'm doing on the job is not an expression of who I am or what I believe, I'm likely to try to fill the emptiness with consumption or seek some exciting new affair.[24] More on that in the next chapter.

GLOBALIZATION FOR NOW

The fast-moving character of Globalization entails that by the time you read this book, a lot might have changed with the economy. But there are clear economic advantages (for some of us). And change along with flexibility are constants with the economy, will be with us for the foreseeable future. Such rapid change manifests itself in individualization and self-concern. For all our friends on Facebook and our networking, you and I are on our own. It's awfully draining, even bewildering. What's life like every day when you live in a globalized ethos? Let's see.

NOTES

1. Thomas L. Friedman, <u>The World Is Flat: A Brief History of the Twenty-First Century</u> (paperback ed.; New York: Pacidor/Farrar, Straus and Giroux, 2007), esp. pp.9ff.

2. <u>Ibid.</u>, pp.200ff.

3. See Richard Sennett, <u>The Corrosion of Character: The Personal Consequences of Work in the New Capitalism</u> (New York: W. W. Norton & Co., 1998), pp.48,63.

4. Friedman, pp.51ff.

5. <u>Ibid.</u>, esp. p.184.

6. <u>Ibid.</u>, pp.243ff.

7. <u>Ibid.</u>, pp.265ff.

8. Also see Brent Waters, <u>Just Capitalism: A Christian Ethic of Economic Globalization</u> (Louisville, KY: Westminster John Knox, 2016), p.52.

9. Friedman, p.252.

10. <u>Ibid.</u>, p.378.

11. <u>Ibid.</u>, pp.286f.

12. <u>Ibid.</u>, pp.273,294.

13. <u>Ibid.</u>, p.516.

14. John Sweller, <u>Instructional Design in Technical Areas</u> (Camverwell, Australia: Australian Council for Educational research, 1999), pp.4-5,11; Eric Kandel, <u>In Search of Memory: The Formation of a New Science of the Mind</u> (New York: Norton, 2006), pp.210,312-315; Nicholas Carr, <u>The Shallows: What the Internet Is Doing To Our Brains</u> (New York and London: W. W. Norton, 2010), pp.124,146-148,193-194; cf. Friedman, p.518

15. Friedman, pp.520-621.

16. Jean Twenge, <u>Generation Me</u> (New York and London: The Free Press, 2006), esp. pp.69ff.

17. Jean Twenge, <u>iGen</u> (New York and London: Atria, 2017), p.169.

18. Friedman, pp.520-521.

19. Ibid., pp.478ff.

20. Cade Metz, "The Gender Gap in Computer Science Research Won't Close for 100 Years," The New York Times, June 21, 2019, based on a study of the Allen Institute

21. Waters, pp.178-179,218.

22. Friedman, pp.339-340,354ff.

23. Sennett, p.23.

24. Ibid., pp.116-117; Christopher Lasch, The Culture of Narcissism: American Life in an Age of Diminishing Expectations (Ne York: W. W. Norton & Co., 1979), esp. pp.122-123.

Chapter 2

EVERYDAY LIFE IN A FLAT WORLD

We've already seen that you've got to be flexible and self-concerned in order to succeed in a flat world. How do these dynamics impact everyday life?

It's a rat-race out there, isn't it? In 2018 American workers logged 1786 hours on the job in a year (8.4 hours a day for male employees). Those numbers ranked us the 8th highest in the world in terms of hours per year worked, behind the likes of South Korea, Mexico, and Costa Rica. The average American in the labor force works hundreds of hours more per year than the Western European work force.

The hours labored are functions of the high levels of productivity of the American worker. And there is a gun at the heads of working men and women to produce. High levels of productivity combined with the most advanced technology are keys to the success of maintaining sufficient living standards in America. Economists project that only if your labor force produces more and is more technologically advanced than other poorer nations will the decent wages Americans have earned since World War II be able to be maintained.[1] That's why jobs which do not demand technological sophistication and have been held in the last decades by workers without a strong work-ethic have been shipped offshore.

This sort of pressure and lifestyle which must ensue from the long hours on the job is not making Americans happy, at least not as content as people in other parts of the world with less thriving economies. A 2020 World Happiness Report published by the United Nations Sustainable Development Solutions Network conducted a study which found that the four happiest nations in the world are those with Socialist economies – Finland, Denmark, Switzerland, and Norway. The USA ranked 18th, far behind Canada, Costa Rica, and The United Kingdom, among others.[2] According to a 2017 survey conducted by Harris Poll, only one-third of Americas claimed to be very happy. And a 2019 Gallup poll indicated that 55% us feel stressed, compared to the global average of only 35%.[3]

There are some good reasons why the new economy is not making Americans happy. Let's return to our analysis in the previous chapter of how business is done in our flat world and apply those insights to the impact such a business ethos has on how people live, behave, and feel.

SUCCESS IN THE FLAT WORLD: HOW THE SYSTEM IS RIGGED AGAINST SOME PEOPLE

We've already noted that in an economy which demands that business be flexible and open to new ideas in order to succeed, where a premium is placed on networking, you need to be creative and have good people skills in order to succeed.[4] Of course, these are commendable personality traits in a culture with a strong sense of community. But in a flat world, in which enduring communities and long-term collaboration can be barriers to economic success, these character traits do not necessarily lead to happiness. As we'll see, recent studies of the human brain indicate that those who live primarily by these values and character traits are not likely to be happy, even if they are successful.

Yes, creativity is a plus in all walks of life. But to be effective and wholesome, creativity and its cousin flexibility require a context. Without such limits, these apparent virtues feed a self-acquisitive Narcissism. And insofar as flexibility and creativity in our new economy connote a willingness to lack attachment, today's business ethos stimulates an individualism which is not tempered by fidelity to others. You need to be careful of such loyalties, lest they undermine your flexibility and ability effectively to compete in the market.

Imagination and creativity are the name of the game. Thomas Friedman notes that the ultimate competitor in getting ahead in the flat world is you yourself. For you must always be open to getting the most out of your imagination as possible, to let nothing impede it.[5] But this entails that we are never really in continuity with ourselves, always needing to re-invent ourselves. The relative success of the Clinton political dynasty in our era, not to mention the Trump phenomenon are clear testimony to the fact that ours is a generation in which reinvention and self-promotion in new contexts are the ideal, not consistency in one's thinking or a consistent life narrative.

The ethos of ever needing to reinvent yourself, of always seeking something new, explains not just the corporate ethos, but also the American labor force's propensity regularly to change jobs. You need to be willing to move on, to take up new challenges, or you'll be deemed and may consider yourself a loser. We get our highs from experiencing what is novel, not sticking to what we have.[6]

Uncertainty about who we are is further exacerbated on the job by the fact that jobs are no longer strictly defined in the new economy. Since what you have done for the company is not as tangible as it was in the old assembly line or sales jobs, your people skills, ability to network, and even to "spin" your contributions to superiors are frequently the key to success. The trick is to be sure that nothing that has been bad for the company is perceived as your fault.

In this context of fluidity and lack of consistency in the way life is lived, people tend to focus on the minutiae of daily events. And so how the boss says hello in the morning or who got invited to dinner become all-important measures of career success.[7] But don't you find in your own life that when you're hung up on the little, even frivolous things of life, it cannot but make you uptight, and so unhappy?

The absence of a clear continuity in one's life story coupled with the fragility of job security due to the flexible ethos of the corporate culture has led to anxiety in the workforce and their immediate superiors. That anxiety has all sorts of insalubrious consequences for the way we live every day, permeating familial relationships, mental health, and purchasing patterns.

We are even anxious about time. Its passage is not our friend, since in the flexible corporation experience is no guide to the present. In fact, time is the enemy of creativity and innovation.[8] These dynamics plug into the youth culture which has dominated the American social psyche at least since the maturation of the Baby Boomers. To labor in the flat world is not much fun (except for the winners, and even they are not immune from anxiety about success).

The new internet technology nurtures flexibility in other ways. It opens ways for working from home, rendering fluid the difference between home and office. We have already noted the fluidity that the flat world seems to afford, the ability to move across class, ethnic, gender, and national lines. Technology makes it possible to move across these lines easily. The issue is whether such ease diminishes the work ethic and engagement in the process in which I participate. When things are fluid, they come easy. But as Sociologist Richard Sennett has suggested, when things are made too easy, we become weak. These dynamics help explain declining standards in much of American society. And when the job is too easy, I am not as much engaged with the job. It becomes superficial.[9] I live for other things; I try to find excitement outside the office or factory. This puts more pressure on families and marital relations to deliver the goods.

Related to this lethargy is the sort of psychological dynamics involved in the consistent use of technology by the American workforce. Intelligence in using machines is dull when the interest is operational rather than self-critical. When I am skilled only in making the machine work, when I am not interested in how the machine affects society and how it might be used differently, or when I am not even willing to challenge its use, my expertise is merely routinized and therefore dulled by routine. I do not need to think; I am no longer challenged. I know <u>how</u> to do things, not <u>why</u> I do them. Computers intensify such dynamics. They provide answers, but not necessarily understanding of the answer provided. I have the answer from the computer without knowing why it is the right answer.

These dynamics entail that I am detached or removed from the work undertaken on the computer. It is not quite mine. I passively receive data or have the mathematical equation figured out for me. I do not have to do much research myself, save my mastery of the machine. With regard to the actual subject of the problem considered, I am a mere spectator, not the problem solver.[10]

Such passivity is not in the interests of the need for creativity and flexibility in American business. It is also not good for society, because, inasmuch I am only loosely connected to the job I do, it does not define me, I really do not know who I am. I have no identity, a trait most symptomatic of the Narcissist.

This sort of passivity likewise manifests itself in the failure of the workforce to understand what it is really doing. The laborer or white-collar administrative assistant does not have the full picture. Indeed, the marked growth of "bull-shit jobs" (administrative positions with little to do save to serve the CEO or be part of her/his hierarchy) embodies how much of the labor force is not invested in what our institutions actually do. Your job-related tasks can't define who you are when you do that kind of work. You're just doing trivial assignments.[11] Not even many of the stockholders really know what is happening in their investments. Even many Board members who represent stockholder interests remain passive in order not to alienate the CEOs and retain their high-paying or prestigious positions. Only the CEOs and select members of their entourage have this vision of how their work relates to the institution's real work or purpose. And knowledge is power.

Bill Clinton's former economic advisor Robert Reich spoke of a culture of meritocracy.[12] But inasmuch as only the managers and the elite have the full picture of what is going on, they have an advantage over the workers, so that their subsequent successes are not really achieved by pure merit. Likewise, the families of the managers also are not likely to be nurtured in the laissez-faire environment of the working class previously described. The flat world definitely works to their advantage. But not for most everybody else.

We've already noted that the creative destruction of old institutions by the globalized economies, so necessary to the flourishing of the flexible global market, entails that some people will be losers, that some jobs must disappear. Flexibility in meeting the ever-changing character of the global market demands it.

The gurus of these economic dynamics respond to these human tragedies with the claim that economic growth must supersede "collateral damage." Everyone will ultimately be helped by these business cycles, they argue, as with more efficiency come lower prices and more good-paying, skilled jobs. What the unemployed or underemployed need to do is to get the skills the winners have and they will gain from these developments too. What these promoters of globalization do not concede is that they have sacrificed the welfare of the displaced laborer who may not be as gifted to learn these new skills for the good of the crowd. Individuals and their well being (especially those the champions of globalization don't know very well) get swallowed up in the welfare of the (richest segments of the) crowd.[13]

OTHER CHARACTER TRAITS FLAT WORLD BUSINESS DYNAMICS NURTURE

In the flat world, we suffer from multiple identity disorder.[14] A good example is how we flock to Wal-Mart for the lower prices, but the compassionate side of each of us deplores the chain's treatment of its labor force (the low wages and minimal benefits). This lack of coherence in our worldview bespeaks another example of the loss of identify that we suffer in the flat world. Not knowing who you are further contributes to our anxiety.

Social critics have suggested that the fact that modern corporate life is predicated on flexibility, not loyalty (for the worker is disposable and the present job just a stepping stone), has deep implications for everyday life. The modern attitude towards divorce and its high numbers can be seen as a reflection of these values learned on the job. If the marriage gets static, it's no good. Besides, our business ethos teaches the workforce to trust themselves, because they can't trust the company. Translated into family life entails that I'll only stay loyal to a spouse unless the relationship feels good to me.[15] Because work no longer defines who I am, the everyday-life manifestation of such uncertainty is that my identity is not readily apparent to me. I need to discover who I am, usually by thrill-seeking and the mad pursuit of novelty.

It is true that modern business management theory does not officially sanction an "I'm on my own" ethos. But the new models have broken with the older top-down systems of hierarchical management in favor of the creation of teams with short tasks.[16] This style of management has in turn led to a downsizing of middle-management jobs (in favor of the peerless, usually interim "bull-shit jobs" previously described).

The modern team is flexible, able to deal with new circumstances and then move on to the next one. In keeping with the egalitarian ethos of post-1960 America and our therapeutic ethos, the team does not acknowledge differences in privileges or power. In our therapeutic ethos, inclined as most Americans are to interpret their lives at least subliminally in the categories of Psychology, conflict is a bad thing. Besides, the team is not designed to last for a long time, but only as long as it meets a specific task. As such, Sociologists note, these teams create a very weak sense of community. For communities in the strong sense are there for the long haul, and they are often strengthened through conflict, for in conflict we work harder at community and establish rules we all share that bind us together.

A related factor is the competition that exists among the labor force in the new economy. In such a context, I cannot really trust my teammates; they are out to get the promotion I want, even to have my job. In such a climate, cooperation on a specific task is not going to nurture friendships and a sense of community. Even in the culture of teamwork characterizing modern management, I am very much alone. In fact, in a culture in which disagreement and conflict are discouraged, the boss can silence my dissent, even co-opting my fellow-workers to his side, leaving me alone to protest without co-workers in my boat (or a labor union) on my side. I am isolated and anxious about life on the job, and so about life off the job. More than likely the anxiety and sense of rootlessness we've been examining is something you've experienced.

The anxiety the American labor force feels as a result of the new economy is not a consequence of our being wimps. Cutting-edge Neuroscience research indicates why the ethos of the flat world and its corresponding impact on everyday American life will not make us happy. Let's take a look at this data in closing.

THE BRAIN'S REACTION TO EVERYDAY LIFE IN THE FLAT WORLD

We need a little more background on the human brain in addition to what was noted in the previous chapter. The brain is comprised of neurons, tiny cells with the ability to communicate with other cells. When they connect with these other cells pathways are created in the brain to perceive nerve signals. Scientists call these connections <u>gray matter</u>. The process of ferrying signals from one brain neuron to another is facilitated by brain chemicals called <u>monoamines</u>. Among the most pleasurable of these neurochemicals are <u>serotonin</u>, which combats depression, and <u>dopamine</u> (a feel-good drug comprised of properties related to amphetamines and cocaine). Dopamine does other good things. In prompting the brain to make new connections it also prepares neurons for novelty (makes us more open to new experiences).

A third pleasurable chemical secreted in the brain under the right circumstances is <u>oxytocin</u>, which triggers deep feelings of love and trust, of a sense of calm well-being and a desire to snuggle. Oxytocin is good for you in other ways. It lowers blood pressure and helps blood vessels expand and contract in order to maintain an even distribution of body heat. It facilitates digestion if stomachs are empty, but retards digestion if they are empty. It lowers stress hormones, but also decreases pain-sensitivity.

Monoamines like dopamine and oxytocin are not freely available to the brain. They are produced in brain cells. In the case of dopamine, it is produced by cells in the ventral tegmental and substantia nigra (cells in the mid-brain). Oxytocin is produced in the base of the brain in a structure termed the hypothalamus. It is connected to the pituitary gland. Once produced, this acid is sent to the pituitary gland, which in turn secretes it to different sections of the brain, especially to a group of cells more in the front of the brain, the nucleus accumbens.

This reference to the saturation of the front of the brain by these drugs is crucial. Research undertaken by the University of Wisconsin-Madison Neuropsychologist Richard Davidson has revealed a link between prefrontal-lobe activity and bliss. Attaching electrodes to his subjects' skulls, Davidson and his colleagues noticed that in reported moments of joy or bliss the prefrontal cortex (especially the left side of the frontal lobe) was most active. There seems to be a corresponding diminution of the activity of the posterior parietal lobe (the neurological region orienting the self in space and time, defining the self's desires).[17]

The frontal cortex (the frontal lobe's gray matter which functions to connect various neurological cells) is the part of our brain charged with operating pro-actively to enhance our well being. As such, it is the segment of the brain responsible for thinking and planning.[18] It seems that when we are engaged in such mental activities, which stimulate the process of connecting the brain's cells, this part of the brain is correspondingly bathed in dopamine.[19] When you are planning or thinking about something bigger than yourself, forgetting your space-time circumstances, you are likely to be happier, because then the prefrontal lobe will become active and get plenty of pleasurable dopamine flowing in your brain.

The implications of this brain research data for understanding the pressures of everyday life in the flat world are evident and profound. As we have seen, in order to succeed in the flat world, you have to be very concerned about your circumstances. Uncertainty about the job makes you very sensitive to cues the boss or your co-workers may subconsciously deliver. You must always be vigilant about the perceptions others on the job have of you. The parietal lobe of the brain is particularly active when you're preoccupied with discerning these cues. Not much proactive planning and thinking transpires in those occasions. Consequently, you don't get much natural dope. Little wonder denizens of the flat world like us are not ecstatically happy people, but are often worn down with anxiety.

Of course, the creativity demanded by the new economy is not in principle an expectation that will lead to unhappiness. When you think creatively there is a good chance that you're connecting more neurons, and so getting your share of feel-good dopamine. But not in a flat world context.

Recall that in flat world economics, you always have to have your eyes on competitors. In other words, the parietal lobe of your brain which orients you in time and space has to be in overdrive. You don't get good natural dope when that part of the brain is in overdrive. And if the parietal lobe is operating along with the prefrontal cortex, you don't get as much dopamine flowing in the part of the brain that receives it. When creativity is on behalf of projects pertaining to yourself, not about something bigger than your own self-interests, you not going to be as happy.

Other social dynamics of life in the flat world exacerbate these dynamics. The abolition of the value of experience and the past in favor of the present is another way of focusing on ourselves and our own self-interests. On such grounds, what I do on the job is to meet present needs, has nothing to do with a tradition or a legacy. And so what I do is only relative to my own space-time circumstances, not to projects bigger than me. As a result, in such a context, the parietal lobe of our brains gets a lot more exercise than the prefrontal lobe, in which case we are likely to be dopamine deprived.

Likewise, the flat world does not encourage relationships as ends in themselves. We are to develop networks (find people who can help us), not just friends. As a result, even relationships are ultimately about ourselves. What we do with our acquaintances and co-workers is ultimately about what we can get out of it. We are not involved in the sort of projects bigger than ourselves which would shut down our parietal lobes and get the dopamine flowing. Little wonder that life in the flat world is less joyful, tinged with anxiety.

The flexibility and corresponding breakdown of life-long commitments in marriage accounts for other pressures and discontent we feel in everyday life in the flat world. Even when dopamine flows and we experience satisfaction in our creativity, the high wears off. The same dynamic is involved in short-term sexual relations, a way of life in the flat world which does not encourage life-long commitments.

Fortunately, our bodies have been blessed with another neurochemical which nurtures long-term sexual relations. I refer to oxytocin, a monoamine which is produced in a structure deep in the base of the brain called the hypothalamus. Once produced, as a result of maternal nursing and snuggling taking place between long-term heterosexual couples, it is sent to the pituitary gland, which in turn secretes the acid to different sections of the brain, especially to a group of cells in the front of the brain. Saturation with this chemical leads to a ferocious attachment of new mothers to their babies, but also similar attachment and contentment between the couples. It seems that the longer a couple is together, the more oxytocin has an impact on parts of the brain which store everyday habits (things you don't forget). And unlike dopamine, it does not appear that you ever develop an immunity to it.[20] Alas the flexibility and extolling of short-term relationships the flat world and our largely narcissistic media promulgate will not let you have much oxytocin. (They even want to take Moms away from their newborn babies as fast as possible in order to get them back into the flat world economic system.)

HOW CAN WE FIND SOME MOUNTAINS?

It has become quite clear again that living flat does not bring much satisfaction, even if it offers more potential to amass wealth. But we human beings are not inclined to change readily, particularly when there are so many incentives (economics, the media messages, inertia) to keep things the same. Besides, we need alternatives for life in the flat world. Friedman has a point. There's no going back to a world that is not flat.

I promised previously that the 19th-century Danish philosopher Søren Kierkegaard might aid us, both in providing insights to help us see how empty life in the flat world as most of us live it is, but also in offering alternatives which will still allow us to engage the new economic realities. In the next chapter, we'll get introduced to Kierkegaard, his vision of three stages of human existence. The first of these stages (the so-called aesthetic stage) helps us understand even more sharply how flat and empty everyday life in the flat world is for most of us. But his other states offer some models for living in the flat world with the same peaks and valleys, with some joy and happiness. Let's proceed.

NOTES

1. Thomas L. Friedman, The World Is Flat: A Brief History of the Twenty-First Century (paperback ed.; New York: Pacidor/Farrar, Straus and Giroux, 2007), esp. pp.400,8,293.

2. Sustainable Development Solutions Network. "World Happiness Report 2020."

3. Harris Poll, "Here's How Happy Americans Are Right Now," at theherrispoll.com>heres-how-happy-americans-are-right-now, accessed March 2, 2020; Gallup 2019 Global Emotions Poll, at www.gallup.com/analytics/248906/gallup-global-emotions-report-2019,asp, accessed April 20, 2020.

4. Friedman, esp. pp.608-609,320ff.

5. Ibid., 634-635.

6. Richard Sennett, The Corrosion of Character: The Personal Consequences of Work in the New Capitalism (New York and London: T. & T. Clark, 1998), p.87.

7. Ibid., pp.78-79.

8. Ibid., pp.96-97.

9. Ibid., p.74.

10. In making these observations I am indebted to by Ibid., pp.74-75.

11. Ibid., p.74; David Graeber, Bull Shit Jobs (New York and London: Simon & Schuster, 2018), pp.163ff.

12. Robert Reich, The Work of Nations (New York: Alfred A. Knopf, 1992).

13. This relegation of job loss and middle-class decline by flat world advocates is evident in Friedman, pp.282ff.; Brent Waters, Just Capitalism: A Christian Ethic of Economic Globalization (Louisville, KY: Westminster John Knox Press, 2016), esp. pp.52,58. Regarding the unfamiliarity that the economy's power brokers have with the working class, see Charles Murray, Coming Apart: The State of White America, 1960-2010 (New York: Crown Forum, 2012).

14. Friedman, pp.250-253.

15. Alan Wolfe, Moral freedom: The Search For Virtue in a World of Choice (New York and London: W. W. Norton & Company, 2001), esp. pp.48-49.

16. Sennett, p.48.

17. See R. E. Wheeler, R. J. Davidson, and A. J. Tomarken, "Frontal Brain Assymetry and Emotional Reactivity: A Biological Substrate of Affective State," Psychophysiologie 30 (1993): 547-558. For this exposition of the new insights in neurobiological research, I am indebted to Stefan Klein, The Science of Happiness: How Our Bodies Make Us Happy – and What We Can Do to Get Happier (New York: Marlowe & Company, 2006), pp.35-37,56-58,107.

18. Dean Hamer, The God Gene (New York: Anchor Books, 2004), p.122.

19. Wheeler, Davidson, and Tomarken, 547-558.

20. Anthony Walsh, The science of Love: Understanding Love and Its Effects on Mind and Body (Buffalo: Prometheus Books, 1991), "I Get a Kick Out of You," The Economist (12 Feb. 2004); Steven Johnson, "Emotions and the Brain: Love," Discover Magazine (May 1, 2003), at http:///discovermagazine.com/2003/may/featlove.

Chapter 3

REMEDY TO OUR DESPAIR: INTRODUCTION TO THE PHILOSOPHY OF SOREN KIERKEGAARD

Many readers have heard of Søren Kierkegaard (1813-1855). For some, this 19th-century Danish author is the founder of Existentialist Philosophy. For others, he was a committed Christian writer embodying the best traditions of Lutheran Pietism. Either way, we regard him as the "solitary individual," concerned with subjective truth. It seems a stretch to think that he could have anything to say to us today about our economic system. Corporate dynamics and concern about people in the street do not seem to have been on this reclusive scholar's radar screen. At least that has been the consensus in large segments of the guild.

But for over 50 years, some Social Scientists and Economists have noted a side of this complex man which is most relevant to the economics of our day. A Nobel Prize-winning Economist, Edmund Phelps, has presented a paper about Kierkegaard's support of the risk-taking it takes to thrive in our globalized economy.[1] On the other hand, in a 1950 paper by Sociologist Werner Stark, connections between the famed Dane and Capitalism are rejected, in favor of an argument for an affinity to Marx.[2] I am sympathetic with these voices to the extent that I agree with them regarding the fact that Kierkegaard's thought has implications for helping us understand and cope with our present socio-economic strands.

Kierkegaard's ideas help us see that caught up as we are in the everyday life of the flat world we may think that we are taking responsibility for ourselves, that in our entrepreneurial activities, we may think we are venturing out on faith, but in fact, these activities are not really expressions of authentic self-concern. For most of the time, our "business" just leads us to losing ourselves or objectifying the people we meet and tweet into the crowd. We have become "ghosts in the global economic and information machines."

With this insight, through an awareness of how meaningless living in flat world conditions has become, how flat and without true passion this style of life is, the great Existentialist can teach us to yearn for more. At least he can prepare us to take leaps of faith into apparently absurd ethical commitments, eventually perhaps into an exciting religious outlook, into passionate lives of highs and lows that can help us quote with our flat world chase for prosperity and instant feedback.

ENCOUNTERING KIERKEGAARD

Let me be very clear. This is not a book about Søren Kierkegaard. It is not a book about the whole of his thought. There are enough academic books on the market to help you sort out those questions or which introduce you to questions about how to interpret him, which we still have not resolved. This is a book about how at least some of Kierkegaard's ideas can help us cope with a flat, interconnected world. Nevertheless, we can still begin with a background on the man and his thought here.

This 19th-century malcontent is usually presented as a solitary individual born with enough money inherited from his successful father that allowed him to spend his life as a writer of controversial books, a man who was regarded as a frivolous rich idler, with a good sense of humor, a man who remained a mystery to his contemporaries in Denmark.[3] But in fact, Kierkegaard seems to have been a man both for the intellectual elite and the masses.

His surname, Kierkegaard, literally means in Danish "church farm" (*kierke gaard*). The younger Kierkegaard was born to a father, Michael Pedersen Kierkegaard (1756-1838), so named because he worked as a tenant farmer in a church farm. (It was still common in Denmark at that time to have the location of your residence become your surname.)

Young Michael Kierkegaard may have started out poor, but his ambition led him to become a rich merchant. But you could not take the country peasant boy out of him, as he is said to have maintained his rural Danish accent and rural style of dress. A child of his father's later years, Søren seems to have inherited both his father's melancholy and also his ability to go home and mix with peasants. He speaks of the sadness he has felt throughout his life since childhood.[4] He regularly mixed with street people in Copenhagen, and enjoyed these engagements. He wrote:

> Being myself of humble origin, I have loved the common people, or what is spoken of as the simple classes... The complaints which have been brought against my mode of life... can only be expressed thus: that I have not shown sufficient regard for my personal dignity, have not been 'superior'; that humanly speaking I have in a light-hearted way (Christianly understood, a God-fearing way) made sport of worldly honor and prestige.[5]

In another context, the first Existentialist noted, "The 'ordinary' person is my task..."[6] If we are to be informed by Kierkegaard in our thinking today we use him illicitly if we do not keep our eyes on the poor and working class.

Kierkegaard is often deployed in Philosophy without reference to what he tells us is primary agenda -- how to become a Christian while living in Christendom.[7] His first and foremost priority was living the Christian life, not with the Existentialist concern with the responsibility of making ourselves who we are by our choices.

The great Existentialist's focus on becoming a Christian is of interest to us, because it is the argument of this book that we can live a happier, fulfilling, exciting life in the flat world when we are in faith. We are people who crave eternal happiness in the midst of our anxious lives today, Kierkegaard once observed, in a manner so timely given the dynamics of contemporary life we have been describing.[8]

Kierkegaard did not advocate for exhorting people to believe these things in his context, nor does he do so in ours. Convinced that this would not yield results in his context, a context in which people had become caught up in objectivity and the mentality of the crowd (he was targeting 19th-century German Idealist G.W.F. Hegel's confidence in Reason), the budding Existentialist believed that we must first arouse self-concern or subjectivity among readers.[9] Subjectivity for Kierkegaard does not refer to the dominance of relativism which characterizes our ethos. It is nothing more than becoming self-concerned. It is taking responsibility for who one is. It involves a passionate commitment to dedicating one's life to how one decides to live, to ensuring that one is related to what is true.[10]

You are most intensely subjective, most full of passion, when you live in paradoxical tension with reason and the objective ways of the world. And subjectivity is heightened further by believing that you find truth in subjectivity – that truth is subjectivity. When that transpires, you are claiming that eternal truth and existence are placed in juxtaposition – the absurd claim is made that what is forever true is found in history.[11]

Kierkegaard proceeds to claim that the maximum experience of subjectivity and the paradox is found in Christianity. For Christian faith claims "to base an eternal happiness upon the relation to something historical..."[12] But if this happiness is found in history, then it seems impossible for it to be eternal. Christianity is the ultimate paradox.

We have now arrived at the real relevance of Kierkegaard for our present context, for this book. A life lived in commitment to Christianity, he teaches, will be a life of passionate rejection of the mores of our flat world. It is a life on the edge, filled with the hope and happiness of eternal truths about God, but in tension with our doubts and anxieties, with the rational uncertainties and paradoxes of faith. It will indeed be a life of peaks and valleys that the title promises. As such, this is a lifestyle in which we really (passionately) "own" our convictions. The 6th Chapter will help you see this more clearly, understanding how the lives of passionate commitment lead to joy and happiness. We'll see how we are biologically constituted to experience more joy when we are passionately committed to what is good.

As he presents the Christian faith, Kierkegaard makes even clearer the paradoxical character of Christian faith, why practicing faith is a risk rejection of our uninspiring, boring life in the flat world. He simply points out the character of Christian faith which all of us can affirm.[13]

First and foremost, the great Danish Philosopher notes, is that the greatest qualitative contradiction is affirmed when Christians claim that God became an individual man. The Incarnation is an "offense" to reason, a contradiction of all that is rational. How can a man be God? As such, this belief cannot but heighten one's subjectivity to its most intense heights.[14] And because it is so offensive to reason, believing in Jesus involves a lot of self-investment in the belief. Because of the yawning difference become God and humanity, it can only be resolved in the situation of contemporaneity. We can only know the God-Man Jesus when we become contemporary with Him. There is no such thing as a disciple at second-hand – no such thing as knowing about Jesus and not knowing and being with Him.[15]

There are other offenses associated with Christian faith. The eternal happiness Christianity affords is related to the terrible, frightful awareness of consciousness of our sin. Christians are aware that they live in a dreadful situation (another example of the peaks and valleys a life of faith offers).[16] In addition, for all the happiness living with an eternal truth affords, the world cannot abide it. And so Christian life involves suffering along with all its joys.[17]

There is an urgency about the moment in Kierkegaard's vision which lends to the excitement we are likely to have about living. Just as in Kierkegaard's Christological formulations (his contention that we must become contemporaneous with Christ – meet Him in the moment), the concept of the Moment is always crucial in his construal of the faith. Just as in a given historical God appeared in time, there is a moment, the Moment, in which individuals, by virtue of the gift of eternal happiness, become aware of their sinful condition and consequent new birth.[18] In this sense, the Moment in time becomes crucial for him:

> But to lose the moment is to become immediate... A moment lost, then,
> is the chain of eternity broken; a moment but, then is the continuity of
> eternity disturbed.[19]

Christians are clearly people who are never bored, with not a moment to waste. The Christian life, on Kierkegaard's grounds, is portrayed as an exciting, risk-taking mode of existence. We'll see in a later chapter how healthy and joyous that way to live is.

Of course, Kierkegaard did not think that the mass of people would begin to seek the Christian form of life in Christendom just by telling them about it, by preaching to them. We need to lure people to appreciate what the Christian form of life offers, showing them how miserable they are in their present mode of existence. Kierkegaard refers to this approach as the Method of Indirect Communication. We need to get people to realize how miserable life is for them now in order to lure them to an appreciation of the benefits of living religiously.[20] But of course ultimately each individual must take their own leap into a new way of living. This strategy dictates the format for this book.

Kierkegaard believed that most people in his context live aesthetically, and that is the reason that they were not receptive to living as Christians. I believe that this is true of most of us living our flat, interconnected world. The aesthetic stage, Kierkegaard contends, is the living of life as turning back to sensuality. Aesthetic people are mere spectators – acting in an unthinking, uncommitted manner. They do what is most readily apparent. Such persons are eminently adaptable to circumstances, seeking enjoyment in order to avoid boredom. They evaluate all things on the basis of whether it is interesting.

Aesthetic living does not involve choice, but is either entirely immediate or loses itself in the multifarious. The aesthete does not define life by choices, for "one chooses only for the moment, and therefore can choose something different the next moment."[21] Aesthetic people do what is natural, avoid commitment, but are ultimately prone to despair. They lack identity because none of their acts defines who they are as individuals.

In the interests of evangelism, Kierkegaard advocated trying to move people off the aesthetic plane to the more ethically oriented mode of existence. Aesthetic people are not subjects, not self-concerned. As such, they will not be ready to hear the Gospel.[22] But since people living at the Ethical stage do have such self-concern, they are likely to be more receptive to a Christian life in which one's commitments define who we are.

Kierkegaard's strategy is related to his concern about nurturing inwardness and subjectivity, his belief in the paradoxical or absurd character of life. He seems much like a 20th-century Existentialist Philosopher at this point. He insists that life lived at each stage is absurd, paradoxical, and so to move from one stage to another is an absurd risk, not a natural evolution or finding oneself.[23] How you live is a choice with no objective justification or rationale. Your choices make you who you are.

The Ethical Stage of Life is a life lived in commitment to a course of action and assuming responsibility for one's own actions. Ethical individuals are no longer mere spectators. Such individuals make free decisions, self-consciously defining who they are. Subjectivity or self-concern is more intense at this stage, for as we have noted, subjectivity does not exist at all for those living aesthetically.[24]

Ethical people come to despair over living a morally perfect life, over oneself and the tension between what one is and what one should be.[25] Kierkegaard calls such despair the "sickness unto death." Religious life becomes an attractive alternative to such people, a way of coping with this despair. Ethical demands condemn one as a sinner and religion provides comfort.[26] Of course, this turning to faith is another offense, requiring an absurd leap of faith to the paradoxical offense that blessedness is based on a relation to something historical.[27] This experience of forgiveness of sin is just one more instance of Christianity's paradoxical claim that you find the eternal in the historical moment and living with that insight!

This book will try to help you make these moves, to help you in Chapter 4 to see and experience how meaningless all our busyness in today's globalized, internet ethos is, how it leads to nothing but a loss of yourself and despair. Then I'll propose what an Ethical way of life today in the flat world might look like, how you might begin to take ownership of your life and not just be a passive consumer of information. One who lives at the ethical stage of life will be a worker who is trying to humanize the workings of the globalized economy, one who endeavors to maintain genuine social solidarity in the face of all the impersonal dynamics which are prevailing on the job and in our personal lives. Of course, then we'll see that such noble efforts to take control of our lives, to right the wrongs of the system, are probably not going to change the world, not even alleviate all the anxieties in our personal lives.

Finally, inspired by Kierkegaard, we will leap to the sixth chapter's description of the Christian life in our flat, interconnected world. With Kierkegaard, we'll observe like he did that the religious stage allows the individual more intense individuality through its sense of immediate relationship to God. The God relationship is so all-consuming that it renders believers oblivious to the finite and its trials. The ethical dimension (the Ethical Stage) is suspended at the Religious Stage.[28] We will see in that chapter that a life lived like Kierkegaard advocates the Christian become will be one lived on high peaks of eternal joys, balanced by the valleys of despair that we all experience when we are living life to its fullest, with all the risks that one takes when living fully. We'll also observe that the results of recent research on the human brain seem to verify how a life spent becoming Christian (in Kierkegaard's sense) can lead to a sense of peaks and valleys in life, experiences that make life a lot better and feel more meaningful (even if it looks more like a life lived on the edges).

Søren Kierkegaard's outlook on life and his agenda to make us become Christian offers profound insights that can inform our socio-economic ethos today, make life in it more tolerable. But scholars have not been using these insights that way -- until this book. Kierkegaard can help us understand why we are not happy, give us a method of addressing our flexible, instant-gratification ways of conducting ourselves. In the rest of this book, we'll be testing these intuitions, and I propose that we'll find that these insights can help us find goodness, truth, and meaning while most everyone else keeps chasing after prosperity and instant feedback.

We'll start with how his insights help us understand ourselves as people living aesthetically. I predict you won't like what you see. Kierkegaard will take our "flat" ways of living into a valley, and then we'll see the peaks on the horizon a little better.

NOTES

1. Edmund Phelps, paper presented at the Columbia Department of Religion and The Center on Capitalism, "Kierkegaard and Economics", 2013.
2. Werner Stark, "Kierkegaard On Capitalism," The Sociological Review 42, No.1 (Jan. 1950): 87-114.
3. Søren Kierkegaard, The Point of View for My Work as An Author: A Report to History, trans. Walter Lowrie (New York, Evanston, and London: Harper & Row, 1962), pp.50-51.
4. Ibid., p.76.
5. Ibid., pp.91-92. Also see Eliseo Pérez-Alvarez, A Vexing Gadfly: The Late Kierkegaard on Economic Matters (Eugene, OR: Pickwick, 2009), p.40.
6. Søren Kierkegaard, Papirer, Vol.X^{2}A, ed. Peter A, Heiberg, Og V. Kuhr, Einar W. Torsting, and Niels Thulstrup (2nd ed.; Copenhagen: Gyldendal, 1968-1978), 48.
7. Søren Kierkegaard, Journal, 5-6,13,42; Søren Kierkegaard, Concluding Unscientific Postscript, trans. David Swenson and Walter Lowrie (Princeton, N.J.: Princeton University Press, 1968), p.13.
8. Søren Kierkegaard, Edifying Discourses: A Selection, ed. Paul Holmer (New York, Evanston, and London: Harper & Row, 1958), p.112.
9. Kierkegaard, Concluding Unscientific Postscript, pp.116ff.
10. Ibid., esp. p.33,115ff., 178.
11. Ibid., pp.187,181-183,191, on paradox.
12. Ibid., pp.345-346,248.
13. It could be argued that as a Lutheran, Kierkegaard is in line here with the Theology of the Cross of Martin Luther, Disputatio Heidelbergae habita (1518), in D. Martin Luthers Werke Kritische Gesamtausgabe (Weimarer Ausgabe), Vol.1 (Weimar: Hermann Böhlaus Nachfolger, 18883), 362,18/ English translation in Luther's Works, Vol.31 (St. Louis-Philadelphia: Concordia Publishing House – Fortress Press, 1955ff.), p.53; Ibid., 354,19/ English translation, Ibid., p.40.

14. Søren Kierkegaard, <u>Training In Christianity</u>, trans. Walter Lowrie (reprint ed.; Princeton, NJ: Princeton University Press, 1971), pp.28,123; Kierkegaard, <u>Concluding Unscientific Postscript</u>, p.209.

15. Søren Kierkegaard, <u>Philosophical Fragments</u>, trans. David Swenson (4th print.; Princeton, NJ: Princeton University Press, 1971), pp.125-137; Kierkegaard, <u>Training In Christianity</u>, pp.66-70.

16. Kierkegaard, <u>Concluding Unscientific Postscript</u>, pp.516-519; Kierkegaard, <u>Training In Christianity</u>, p.71.

17. Kierkegaard, <u>Training In Christianity</u>, pp.36,221; Kierkegaard, <u>Concluding Unscientific Postscript</u>, p.529.

18. Kierkegaard, <u>Philosophical Fragments</u>, pp.25-26

19. Søren Kierkegaard, "Our Duty To Remain in the Debt of Love to One Another," <u>Works of Love</u>, trans. David Swenson and Lillian Marvin Swenson (Princeton, N.J.: Princeton University Press, 1946), p.148.

20. Kierkegaard, <u>The Point of View for My Work as An Author: A Report to History</u>, pp.24-26; Kierkegaard, <u>Concluding Unscientific Postscript</u>, pp.261-262.

21. Søren Kierkegaard, <u>Either/ Or</u>, Vol.II, trans. Walter Lowrie (Princeton, N.J.: Princeton U niversity Press, 1944), pp.171,223,234.

22. <u>Ibid.</u>, p.223.

23. Kierkegaard, <u>Concluding Unscientific Postscript</u>, pp.261ff.

24. Kierkegaard, <u>Either/ Or</u>, Vol.II, pp.196,233-234.

25. <u>Ibid.</u>, pp.199,212-213,222-223.

26. <u>Ibid.</u>, pp.223-244; Søren Kierkegaard, <u>The Sickness Unto Death</u>, trans. Walter Lowrie (3rd. prin.; Princeton, NJ: Princeton University Press, 1970), pp.251-252; Kierkegaard, <u>Concluding Unscientific Postscript</u>, pp.516-518.

27. Kierkegaard, <u>Concluding Unscientific Postscript</u>, pp.518-519; cf. Kierkegaard, <u>The Sickness Unto Death</u>, pp.253-254.

28. Kierkegaard, <u>Concluding Unscientific Postscript</u>, pp.433-441.

Chapter 4

AESTHETIC LIFE: DESCENDING INTO
THE FLAT WORLD'S VALLEYS

Kierkegaard began his career as an author writing books anonymously which aimed to explore the Aesthetic Stage of Life and how it might relate to the Ethical Stage.[1] We've already talked a little about the Aesthetic Stage. Let's see if Kierkegaard is right about this being the mode of existence for most of us today.

Aesthetic people live life as turning back to sensuality. They are mere spectators, acting in an unthinking, uncommitted manner. Is this not in line with the need to be flexible in order to succeed in our globalized context? Don't think about long-range implications for your business or career. And don't plan on keeping in touch with everyone in your network your whole life, not even a spouse. We've already noted how many American workers are likely to find themselves in several different jobs in a career. The Bureau of Labor Statistics reported in 2019 that the average number of jobs we hold in a lifetime is 12. And 2019 FactTank Study found that 4 in 10 marriages is a remarriage. This is related to the fact that 39% of all marriages end in divorce, as per a Time Magazine report in 2018. Has Kierkegaard not characterized the way a lot of us are living in the flat world when he says we are living aesthetically?

Wait: The connections with everyday life are even more striking. Kierkegaard contends that people living aesthetically are "existential possibilities," experimenting with life, almost childlike. They are not really actualized human beings, not fixed or firm in some identity like someone who lives ethically.[2] Everything is possible, denizens of the flat world are told. We're always inventing and re-inventing ourselves. This is the essence of the successful, flexible worker in the globalized business world.

The father of Existentialism elaborates further on the characteristics of the Aesthetic man or woman. He writes: "Aesthetically it is quite in order to wish for wealth, good fortune, and the most beautiful of damsels... "[3] Isn't this what life is all about in the flat world? Gaining wealth is what life is all about, and will help your career and make it. A 2019 Cato Institute reported that 71% of us admire the rich. And studies indicate that a beautiful mate enhances one's social standing.

The reference to wishing for beauty is a reminder that eros, erotically pursing beauty is what living Aesthetically is all about. Such a person is like a seducer.[4] And so today the men and women of our flat world here in America (esp. younger generations) have created the Hook-Up Culture. A 2018 study by Euroclinix found that the medium average number of sex partners for Americans was between 10 and 16 partners. A University of Colorado Department of Psychology study found that from 2000 to 2016, about 21 percent of men and 13 percent of women reported infidelity at some point in their lifetime. Kierkegaard's fictional seducer writes these words after his conquest:

> Still, it is over now, and I hope never to see her again... I do not wish to be reminded of my relation to her; she has lost her fragrance...[5]

And so likewise many of us move on to the "next chapter" of our lives, never seeking or caring much about harmony or narrative continuity in our lives among life's chapters. The significant other, the job, or the colleagues are of the past are only of value insofar as they *were* good for us Kierkegaard's reflections on marriage understood Aesthetically could have been written for today's critiques of institution of marriage or for the unhappy lover looking for an out:

> Husband and wife are indeed said to become one, but this is a very dark and mystic saying. When you are one of several, then you have lost your freedom; you cannot send for your travelling boots whenever you wish, you cannot move aimlessly about in the world... it is likely to be tiresome in the long run – for the husband. Marriage brings one into the fatal connection of custom and tradition, and traditions and customs are like the wind and weather, altogether incalculable.[6]

Friendship is nearly as bad, Kierkegaard adds.

One who lives aesthetically is filled with lust, with a lust for pleasure. He has lost himself or herself. Such a person hides in the moment of pleasure.[7] Even work seems foolish, a waste of one's time, so meaningless:

> Of all the ridiculous things, it seems to me the most ridiculous is to be a busy man of affairs, prompt to meals, and prompt to work... And who could not help laughing? What do they accomplish, these hustlers?[8]

Kierkegaard found these dynamics, so suggestive of life in the 21st century, not expressions of evil. Rather life in this context is just blah, flat. For all our quest for pleasure and the latest "high" we can experience, our lives really are emotionally and intellectually flat:

Let others complain that the age is wicked; my complaint is that it is paltry; for it lacks passion. Men's thoughts are thin and flimsy like lace, they are themselves pitiable like lacemakers.[9]

The famed Existentialist seems to know us well. In a flat world, we crave passions – highs and lows. But most of the time in our globalized, interconnected context, life feels pretty flat and routine, does it not? Rather than feeling excited and energetic, we often feel burned out.

BOREDOM:
TRAPPED IN LIFE'S VALLEYS WITHOUT THE GOOD BRAIN DOPE

What accounts for the miseries of post-modern life? It is not as simple as blaming it all on globalization. A 2019 poll by market research firm OnePoll found that most Americans spend 1/3 of their day bored. Kierkegaard's analysis speaks to this data. In his view, the core problem in the life of the Aesthetic man or woman is that "all men are bores."[10] Children are well behaved until they get bored. Indeed it is said to be the root of all evil. The effort to avoid the emptiness of boredom is what drives the Aesthetic man or woman. We move on to the next challenge in our career, we remain flexible, even in our relationships, because the new job, lover, challenge might titillate us, keep us fresh. But it will not make us happy, Kierkegaard says.

Neurobiology offers insights about why not. We need to be reminded here of the role of monoamines, brain chemicals which facilitate the connections between brain cells. The most talked about these days is an amphetamine-like monoamine termed **dopamine**. Like any amphetamine you get a high from this chemical.

As already noted, the main dopamine pathways run through the front part of the brain (the frontal cortex). When this part of the brain (the brain's administrative region, also involved when we are engaged in intellectual and spiritual pursuits) is activated, we are rewarded with this good-feeling chemical which also enhances our energy and heightens our sense of anticipation for engaging it its associated activities. But dopamine does not run through the back part of our brains (the parietal lobe), This brain lobe plays important roles in integrating sensory information from various parts of the body, knowledge of numbers and their relations, and in the manipulation of objects. Its function also includes processing information relating to the sense of touch and visual processing. This part of our brain (the animal part of the brain) needs to be in overdrive on the job, where responding to social cues is essential for the relational skills we need to thrive in a Team Management ethos. As we've noted, then, concentration on these tasks and keeping an eye on the competition, working regularly on the internet with all its visual and audio distractions, focusing on your own self-interest is not as likely to make you happy or energetic.

The dopamine is not as likely to flood your brain.[11]

In addition, the parietal lobe is activated in sexual arousal, when we are excited by how a potential lover looks.[12] Given the exacerbated role, this part of our brains needs to play in our globalized, interconnected ethos, this may explain why sexual infidelity and hooking-up are so fashionable in our ethos. Of course, when you are just aroused, it does not begin all that much pleasure. We'll talk in the next chapter about the dynamics of sexual pleasure which are associated with dopamine and another good-feeling brain chemical oxytocin, the latter of which is experienced especially in long-term heterosexual relations.

No less exciting is the discovery of the parietal lobe's role in artistic production.[13] This entails that people living Aesthetically on Kierkegaard's suppositions also have active parietal lobes. This is one more indication of the viability of applying the Existentialist thinker's analysis of the Aesthetic Stage to the way most of us are living today, explains why so many of us are not really happy and content in the flat world. Likewise, the active role the parietal lobe plays in living aesthetically and its role in sexual arousal links with Kierkegaard's relating the Aesthetic Stage to sexual seduction.

Of course, you do get dopamine saturating your brain in sexual intercourse and intimacy as well as when you try or learn new things. And we can get an amphetamine effect from the use of certain hard drugs, which Americans have less and less difficulties obtaining or less and less inhibitions using. Why then are Americans ranked so low in happiness in comparison to other nations? And other studies have shown that the Millennial Generation, for whom globalization and internet connectivity are the only way of life they have known, poll as less happy than older generations.[14] Brain research helps us sort out these data as well. First, we need to note that you get more dopamine the more active the frontal lobe is in your thinking and experiencing. But when my latest project (a novel task connected with my job, an artistic creation, or sex) is related to me and my needs, then the flow of dopamine is not as rich as in the case of projects in which I lose myself in the activity. For the most concentrated area of dopamine receptors in the human brain is in the frontal and temporal lobes, not the parietal lobe.

We need to remember that dopamine is an amphetamine, and so like any amphetamine, we can get addicted. That is, the more times we enjoy the dopamine secreted in connection with some new project or undertaking, the more habitual it is, the less pleasurable it becomes, because the quantity of dopamine required to heighten anticipation becomes greater and greater until we are not receiving enough to get high.[15]

Kierkegaard was correct in his analysis, it seems. Aesthetic living in the flat world leads to a sense of the passionless meaninglessness. He writes, "How absurd men are!... My view of life is utterly meaningless." There is no happiness for one who lives aesthetically.[16]

What keeps us moving then? Why are we so busy? It all goes back to boredom, Kierkegaard says:

> Boredom is the root of all evil... The influence it exerts is altogether magical, except that it is not the influence of attraction, but of repulsion... so strange is the way of the world, so pervasive the influence of habit and boredom, that this is practically the only case in which the science of aesthetics receives its just dues.[17]

The first Existentialist proceeds to explain how it is boredom which moves the husband to seek divorce, leads the public to seek new political leaders. And then he adds:

> ... we can only annul boredom by enjoying ourselves – *ergo* it is our duty to enjoy ourselves... The second form of boredom is usually the result of a mistaken effort to find diversion. The fact [is] that the remedy against boredom may also serve to produce boredom...[18]

Bored as we are, we need to kill time with shopping, with the latest video game, enroll in the latest Streaming Service that the most recent Facebook posts say I've got to have, join the status country club, take some diners at that four-star restaurant, get that six-figure home in the better neighborhood, and maybe even "grow" by cultivating new relationships or even enter a new "chapter" in my intimate liaisons or family life. The old is so boring. I need to stay fresh.

It's certainly good for the economy, cultivates my flexibility. But as we've noted, the polling data indicates that life in the globalized, ever-changing, find-new-things world it is not making us happy.

Kierkegaard hints as to why we can never find real happiness living aesthetically. We're all bores, he claims. Boring to ourselves, we likely bore others. But we join the crowd hoping others and their activities will be of interest. Those who put off the boredom by keeping busy are certainly boring to others.[19]

When you live aesthetically, how you feel at the moment, your mood determines who you are. But that means, as we previously noted, that you are not really defined, don't know who you are since you and your mood are always changing. Kierkegaard put it this way:

> For he who lives aesthetically seeks as far as possible to be absorbed in mood; he seeks to hide himself entirely in it, so that there remains nothing in him which cannot be inflected into it; for such a remainder has always a disturbing effect. The more the personality disappears in twilight of mood, so much the more is the individual in the moment, and this, again, is the most adequate expression for the aesthetic existence: it is in the moment.[20]

Live for the moment, as the Baby Boom Generation said in its youth. But as Kierkegaard proceeded to note, this leads to one oscillation after another, to a lack of continuity in one's life and sense of self.[21]

Neurobiologists have observed that being scattered in this way entails the brain connections rooted in our frontal lobes associated with sustained concentration are weakened.[22] As a result of these brain dynamics, those of us living in the flat world, are prone to decreased attention span, apathy, and poor on mood control. Procrastination, test and social anxiety, mood control problems, and not inclined to share feelings.[23] If these characteristics seem to describe you, studies of brain function indicate that it is likely because you have become the ideal worker/consumer in the flat world – flexible, and pleasure-seeking. And when the part of your brain regulating healthy behavior is more dormant, then as we've noted, you don't get the good-feeling brain chemical dopamine secreted which makes you happy. In fact, the shutdown of the prefrontal cortex can even increase the likelihood of depression.[24]

NOTHINGNESS – AND WHAT TO DO ABOUT IT

Don't feel too bad about yourself if you find yourself or your friends in this description. (And if you don't, be sure you've been honest with yourself about how you've been living.) All the dynamics of flexibility, lack of respect for lessons of the past, glorifying what's new, individualization, and self-concern (bordering on Narcissism) reflect in the market and are glorified by the media (including social media). We want all these things so badly, all the new things and experiences, in order to avoid boredom. But we're bored, Kierkegaard says, because we're empty. Boredom is characterized by emptiness.[25]

Of course, we're empty in the flat world. We've forfeited who we are in order to keep up with the latest trends. We're just going with the flow, the meaningless, with no real sense of self which allows us to master the ever-changing flow, which each day brings us closer to the end of it all.[26] As Kierkegaard once put it, while lamenting how little pleasure our joys and the striving for them bring for one who spends all his her time striving for it:

> I do not care for anything... I do not care at all. There are well-known insects which die in the moment of fecundation. So it is with all joy; life's supreme and richest moment of pleasure is coupled with death.[27]

We've already talked about the Neurobiological reasons for our unhappiness in the flat world and also noted that most Americans do not poll as happy. The famed Existential Philosopher wrote some remarks that may capture how you or your acquaintances may feel as we run the busy rat-race of the flat world, seeking some pleasure from internet connections:

> Wine can no longer make my heart glad; a little of it makes me sad, much makes me melancholy. My soul is faint and impotent; in vain I prick the spur of pleasure into its flank... I have lost my illusions. Vainly I seek to plunge myself into the boundless sea of joy; it cannot sustain me, or rather I cannot sustain myself.[28]

> So I have reached the point where you affirm that the meaning of life is sorrow... Our age, moreover, has in so many way had experience of the vanity of life that it does not believe in joy, and so to have something to believe it, it believes in sorrow.[29]

And so our age is resigned to being burned out, being tired, and complaining about it. It's about depression and despair. Lives dedicated to finding pleasure and seeking oneself, to the pursuit of money, power, and influence, find nothing but emptiness and so despair. We've already noted how Kierkegaard describes the essence of aesthetic living in terms of wishing for "wealth, good fortune, and the fairest of damsel." An eternal happiness is not on the radar screen.[30] This explains why polls indicate that while religious affiliation in American declines so is the spiritual sense among the youngest generations. [31] No point in preaching God's Word to folks caught up in this mindset. This is why if we want to help people thrive in the flat world (and I think living religiously in the Christian sense is the best option) we need first to help them appreciate how miserable they are living Aesthetically and to experience for themselves that they won't find much more contentment in the other options.

As Kierkegaard himself, speaking for one living Aesthetically put it: "How barren is my soul and thought... My life is absolutely meaningless."[32] Of course, we do not want to admit this to ourselves. That would involve more self-reflection (Kierkegaard calls it "subjectivity) that denizens of the flat world want to admit. Such a realization would move us towards a valley, which those of us devoted to sensuality, living in the moment, Narcissistic in our engagements and image-conscious do not want to engage. No, we Baby Boomers, X-ers, Millennials, and x-Geners are out to have a good time, want to create an image of being well-adjusted. But of course, it's all an empty, self-serving, self-deceiving ruse. Kierkegaard writes:

> So here we have a view of life which teaches one to enjoy life but expresses it thus: "Enjoy yourself, in enjoyment it is yourself you must enjoy..." In this case the condition requisite for enjoyment is after all an outward one which is not within the control of the individual, for although he says he enjoys himself, yet he enjoys himself only in the enjoyment, but the enjoyment is dependent upon an outward condition.[33]

Having fun in a flat world is so precarious, not a high, since in the ever-changing world of globalization what is making us happy can be taken away anytime (or we'll get bored with it). Is that not life as we experience it too often? How meaningless and empty all our business and hustling for pleasure and status seem. It cannot but produce a sense of depression (why so many of us in the flat world are depressed) and melancholy (Kierkegaard's term for describing life in the flat world). The famed Existentialist so well describes our plight:

> Or is not melancholy the defect of our age? Is it not this which resounds even it its frivolous laughter? Is it not melancholy which has deprived us of courage to command, of courage to obey, or power to act, of the confidence necessary to hope?[34]

What do we do about this melancholy, occasioned by the nothingness of life in the flat world, the cycles of boredom and distraction we need to move on? Kierkegaard's whole plan is not to tell you or me what to do. He does suggest that we think about the despair and melancholy resulting from Aesthetic existence in the flat world. Are you feeling these feelings? He says that he merely wants to tear us loose from all our illusions about how joyful and creative life is in the flat world – how we're just dependent on the latest highs, social trends, the power/influence we can yield, or passing moods. Kierkegaard is trying to get you and me to recognize our despair, because "then never more will your frivolity cause you to wander like an unquiet spirit, like a ghost, amid the ruins of as world which to you is lost." In such despair, we can begin to overcome melancholy and the world might become beautiful and joyful as we soar up into the world of freedom![35]

Leaping Away From Aesthetic Life

How can a sense of emptiness, melancholy, and despair move us towards the highs of seeing life as joyful and beauty? If this chapter has created some uneasiness about the way you have been living, has helped name the discontent and fears you have been feeling, then you intuitively know what Kierkegaard means. You've begun to see that Aesthetic living is falling short. Helped by Kierkegaard's analysis you have begun to wish you had an alternative. Looking at your life in the flat world, recognizing life is not so much flat as it is being lived in a depressing, empty valley may have created a yearning for some (Ethical) mountaintops to climb in our flat world.

Kierkegaard's analysis really teaches us that there are "Either/Ors" in life. Either we are content with our aesthetic existence or we look for another (ethical) way to live. But a decision must be made, and it is up to you and me. Once we begin to take decisions the individual has become inward, self-directing and not determined by the moment or the latest external development. It is a choice to be oneself, not determined by what is outside oneself, by the latest post, social trend, or mood. In this connection, Kierkegaard claims that "subjectivity, inwardness, is truth."[36] If you are sensing unhappiness, despair, or melancholy about life in the flat world, dipped into that valley, then the next chapter offers you an alternative which might just provide you with a flat world peak and some peace of mind.

NOTES

1. Søren Kierkegaard, Concluding Unscientific Postscript, trans David F. Swenson and Walter Lowrie (Princeton, NJ: Princeton University Press, 1941), p.224.
2. Ibid., pp.262-263,284-285; Søren Kierkegaard, Either/Or, Vol.II, trans Walter Lowrie (Princeton, NJ: Princeton University Press, 1944), pp.266-267.
3. Kierkegaard, Concluding Unscientific Postscript, p.351.
4. Søren Kierkegaard, Either/Or, Vol.I, trans David F. Swenson and Lillian M. Swenson (Princeton, NJ: Princeton University Press, 1944), pp.43ff.,297ff.
5. Ibid., p.439.
6. Ibid., p.293.
7 Ibid., Vol.II, pp.234-235.
8. Ibid., Vol.I, p.24.
9. Ibid., p.27.
10. Ibid., p.281.
11. See Nicholas Carr, The Shallows: What the Internet Is Doing To Our Brains (New York and London: W. W. Norton, 2011).
12. Nicoletta Cera, Ezio Di Peirro, Francesco Gambi, et al, "The role of the left superior parietal lobe in male sexual behavior: dynamics of distinct components revealed by FMRI," The Journal of Sexual Medicine (June 9, 2012: 1602-1612).

13 Ambar Chakravarty, "The neural circuitry of visual artistic production and appreciation: A proposition," <u>Annals of Indian Academy of Neurology</u> 15, No. 2 (April-June, 2012): 71-75;

14. Jean Twenge, <u>iGen: Why Today's Super-Connected Kids Are Growing Up Less Rebellious, More Tolerant, Less Happy – and Completely Unprepared for Adulthood</u> (New York and London: Simon & Schuster, 2017).

15 Robert Sapolsky, <u>Behave: The Biology of Humans at Our Best and Worst</u> (New York: Penguin, 2017), pp.69-70

16. Kierkegaard, <u>Either/Or</u>, Vol.I, pp.19,24,39.

17. <u>Ibid.</u>, pp.281-282.

18. <u>Ibid.</u>, p.286.

19. <u>Ibid.</u>, pp.284,286.

20. <u>Ibid.</u>, Vol.II, p.234.

21. <u>Ibid.</u>

22. Carr, pp.141-142,194

23. Daniel Amen, <u>Change Your Brain, Change Your Life</u> (New York: Three Rivers Press, 1998), esp. p.116.

24. <u>Ibid.</u>, p.43; Carr, p.194.

25. Kierkegaard, <u>Either/Or</u>, Vol.I, p.287.

26. <u>Ibid.</u>, Vol.II, pp.234-235.

27. <u>Ibid.</u>, Vol.I, p.20.

28. <u>Ibid.</u>, p.40.

29. <u>Ibid.</u>, Vol.II, p.239.

30. Kierkegaard, <u>Concluding Unscientific Postscript</u>, p.351.

31. Twenge, <u>iGen</u>, pp.130ff.

32. Kierkegaard, <u>Either/Or</u>, Vol.I, pp.23,35.

33. <u>Ibid.</u>, Vol.II, p.195.

34. <u>Ibid.</u>, p.24.

35. <u>Ibid.</u>, p.223.

36. Kierkegaard, <u>Concluding Unscientific Postscript</u>, p.266; Kierkegaard, <u>Either/Or</u>, Vol.II, p..173.

Chapter 5

ETHICAL LIFE: CONSTRUCTING SOME PEAKS AND FINDING SOME JUSTICE IN A FLAT WORLD

Where does someone go to when it's become clear that living for the moment and for pleasure (living aesthetically) in our flat world is a dead end? As I noted in the last chapter, if you are asking that question, you have already begun to take more ownership over your life, started to take a leap to another way of living. Kierkegaard calls it the Ethical Stage. What does he mean by the Ethical Stage, what does it look like, and how can you live that way in the flat world? Let's see.

In a way, it's common sense. As we've previously noted, the Ethical Stage on Life's Way is a life lived in commitment to a course of action and assuming responsibility for one's own actions. Ethical individuals are no longer mere spectators of their own lives, like people who live aesthetically are. Let's get into a little more detail about what Kierkegaard means by living Ethically and also why many Americans are hungry to try to live this sort of life.

THE ETHICAL LIFE: KIERKEGAARD'S VERSION

Richard Sennett, a Sociologist who has carefully analyzed life in the new globalized economy, offers some remarks which set the stage for understanding the need for an Ethical style of life in our globalized ethos. He writes:

> When a person lacks belief that anything can be done to solve the problem, long-term thinking can be suspended as useless. However, focal attention may remain active. In this state, people will turn over and over again the immediate circumstances in which they are caught, aware that something needs to be done even though they do nothing...

> For a human being, the aftermath of an act of risk can lead to suspended focal attention of the same sort. "Never getting anywhere," "always at square one," confronted by seemingly meaningless success or the

impossibility of reward for effort; in all these emotional states, time seems to grind to a halt; the person in these toils becomes prisoner of the present, fixated on its dilemmas.[1]

Sennet well describes the plight of one who lives aesthetically. His comments also explain a lot of the present economic developments of globalization, the infatuation of businesses with short-term profits and the latest stock value over long-terms profitability. What's the alternative? Not living in the moment, doing long-term thinking. This is in large part what Kierkegaard means by the Ethical Stage of Life.

The great Existentialist forerunner makes the contrast between Ethical and the Aesthetic style of life in one of his later, distinctively Christian works:

The aesthetic and intellectual principle is that no reality is thought or understood until its *esse* [being] has been resolved into its *posse* [potentiality]. The ethical principle is that no possibility is understood until each its *posse* has really become an *esse*. An aesthetic and intellectual scrutiny protests every *esse* which is not a *posse*; the ethical scrutiny results in the condemnation of every *posse* which is not an *esse*, but this refers only to a *posse* in the individual himself, since the ethical has nothing to do with the possibilities of other individualities. [2]

The point is that while life for one living Aesthetically is all about seeking potential, that life is focused on what might be. As a result, one lives with flexibility, ever-changing, never really defining who one is. By contrast, one living ethically is committed to definite moral principles. It does no good simply to reflect on what might be regarding values (their possibility). You need to realize those values in life!

Another way to talk about the difference between living ethically and living aesthetically surfaces in this quotation. The Aesthetic person lives according to immediacy, to one's mood. And as Richard Sennett observed above, that gets you nowhere. It can make you feel like everything you do means nothing, that you're just spinning your wheels. This is the frustration of life in the flat world which the previous chapter described.

Living the ethical way of life, by contrast, in Kierkegaard's view entails saving oneself from the present moment with a commitment to mastering one's lust for pleasure! Not that the desire for pleasure or lust is gone. But it does not dictate to the individual who she or he is. Who a person is is no longer diffused. Rather who I am is at the center of what I do. It determines who I am. This is what Kierkegaard means by becoming subjective. The individual determines himself/herself, is no longer the object of the winds of change or mood.[3]

Another way Kierkegaard puts it: The Ethical individual has chosen himself/herself.[4] When you've made this choice, you resolve no longer to allow the winds of change, the latest mood, to define who you are. The dynamics of the job, making sure I keep my connections and relationships good even if the boss asks me to do something unethical, or my latest passion and mood no longer determine who I am. I have chosen certain values of good and morality which determine me and my behavior!

Kierkegaard makes this point by claiming that for one who lives in the Ethical Stage, the ethical reality of the individual is the only reality.[5] Unlike one who lives aesthetically, when everything else is gone, at least the Ethicist has herself/himself[6]. Even when the job has hit a dead end, when the power and influence I had is lost, the fleeting joy I had with the latest gadget or exciting new venture is gone and it all feels so boring, at least I still have myself and a commitment to doing and being good. Ethical individuals still have their intimate relationships and friendship intact even when they do not seem to be meeting their immediate needs. Even if this job or assignment sucks, I'll stick it out and get it done. While for the Aesthete, joy is a function of what is outside oneself (if I have that job, that much sought-after trinket, that relationship with someone powerful or beautiful), for one living Ethically, happiness is a matter of whether you can live with yourself.[7]

Elsewhere Kierkegaard claims that joy is social.[8] There is no contradiction here, for one living Aesthetically, depending on what is outside oneself for happiness, is not really being social. Such a person is all alone, using what is outside merely as a tool for happiness. While for one living at the Ethical Stage of Life true joy happens with other people, when he or she is doing something with or for others. This insight correlates with the latest insights of Neurobiology and Evolutionary Theory. It is always better to do something with or for other people. For in social situations, our prefrontal cortex (the front part of our brains) is activated, and as we've previously noted, when that happens, your brain is saturated with that good-feeling brain chemical dopamine.[9] Social engagement makes you happy.

Is This What Flat World People Want?

Some poll data suggests that there might be a yearning in the flat world for something like the Ethical Stage, a sense that we might need it. In a 2019 Gallup poll, 47% of us rate U.S. moral values as "poor" and another 36% of Americans as only "fair."[10] It seems that a significant number of us question Aesthetic life, wonder if it is causing us to lose ethical, moral values. Indeed many of us seem to feel that we need a rekindling of Ethical thinking and living. Americans also poll as hungry for this morality personally, since, according to a 2017 Pew Research Center report, 69% of us say family is what provides the greatest sense of meaning in life, compared to only 34% saying this about our careers and 23% claiming this about money.[11] Further investigation of Kierkegaard's portrayal of the Ethical State of Life provides even more insight regarding what Ethical living in the flat world might look like and why you might want it for yourself. Kierkegaard's elaborations also instruct you and me how to live this way in our globalized context.

LIVING ETHICALLY IN A FLAT WORLD

Kierkegaard notes that Ethical people are both bolder and perhaps more content (at least better able to cope with the chaos of globalization) than people who live aesthetically. One of the reasons is that although ethical individuals are more subjective, resolved not to let the things of the world shake a sense of who he or she is, an ethically rooted individual is not in solitude, but engaged in a civic life.[12] You can't practice Ethics only in solitude. It involves engagement with others, and as previously noted such engagement is likely to make life happier.

What does all this mean for everyday life on the job in a flat world or in the home? Kierkegaard relates the Ethical Style of Life to work. He has the ethical individual state, "What every man accomplishes and can accomplish is to do *his* job in life."[13] In fact, reflecting very Scandinavian values (as any child of Vikings will attest), he adds that the Ethical viewpoint regards it as a human being's *duty* to work.[14] (Ethical) life is all about doing your duty! To be Ethical is obviously then not necessarily a barrier to success in the globalized world. Even Thomas Friedman has lamented a loss of a work ethic, a growing sense of entitlement, among many Americans. He worries about our becoming more consumers than workers. And that will not serve us well in the globalized environment.[15] And there is a growing percentage of men who have given up on the job market, are not even seeking work. Many younger members of the Millennial Generation poll as determined not to let work define them, as believing that there are other things in life except work.[16]

Ethical people also make better spouses, parents, and community members. They do not allow their moods to dictate their behavior, for the commitments of one's person outweighs the latest moods. Such individuals will go and vote or join the social movement even if the weather is bad and he or she does not feel like getting involved.[17] Such individuals will not give up on that child, not give up on that marriage, no matter how frustrating or unfulfilling it feels.

Why? Are ethical individuals masochists? Sort of. But not exactly. Remember how boring, unfulfilling, and empty an Aesthetic life involving the meaningless pursuit of pleasure and beauty is.

Kierkegaard adds that the Ethical individual understands life, understands the duties as callings:

> The ethicist speaks briefly: "It is every man's duty to have a calling.".... What the ethicist can teach him [the Aesthetic person] is that there is a calling for every man, and when our hero has found his the ethicist can admonish him to choose it ethically.. The ethical thesis that every man has a calling is the expression for the fact that there is a rational order of things.[18]

When you are doing your duty, realize that you have to work to live, you are in touch with the rational order of things. As such, the job is not just a "dumb job," the voting, civil participation, and maintaining the marriage are not just meaningless undertakings. They matter! These are duties that are part of the universal order of the cosmos, no matter how insignificant they seem or feel![19]

This way of looking at your job and other duties makes them beautiful, even a pleasure. Kierkegaard writes:

> The ethical consideration that everyone has a calling possesses a double advantage over the aesthetic theory of talent. In the first place, it explains [*forklarer*] talent not as something accidental in existence but as the universal; in the second place, it exhibits the universal in its beauty. For talent is beautiful only when it is transfigured [*forklaret*] as a call, and existence is beautiful only when everyone has a call.[20]

From what we know about Neurobiology, this insight makes sense. Since the 19th century, it has been observed that moral instincts seem rooted in the frontal lobe of the human brain. And we also know that this part of the brain is activated when we meditate on engagement in a reality bigger than we are (like the universal or a rational order of things).[21] This fits the appreciation that when that lobe of the brain is active, we enjoy the flow of the good-feeling brain chemical dopamine, which is associated with sociality.[22] Sex and love are also better biologically for the Ethical individual committed to lifetime and faithfulness to a lover and/or a friend. You not only get the good-feeling brain chemical dopamine secreted in your brain, but another salubrious chemical, oxytocin. More of that in closing.

Living ethically certainly has its advantages. Kierkegaard proceeds to observe that for one living Ethically, the job (duties) outweighs your mood.[23] Sure you will feel all the pleasures, even the sense of meaninglessness or boredom. Suffering will also be experienced (as we'll see, it is even a necessary component of the Religious Style of Life).[24] But they do not have the last word for ethical individuals, because they know who they are and their duties outweigh passing feelings. What is important for such individuals is what you accomplish, not just the feelings of satisfaction you get when unfolding your talent, as the Aesthete says.[25] Work is a pleasure under such circumstances, because for the ethical human being, it is the fulfillment of the duties of his or her calling.[26] If what you do is who you are, then you'll never have to work a day of your life.

There are other payoffs for living ethically. Resolve to start looking at life in terms of duty, to see your job, your community and your family responsibilities as duties, and consider these additional advantages for everyday life. When you are no longer torn and swayed by the latest mood, but your moods are subordinated to your subjective identity (your sense of who you are, your duties), then there is continuity in your life. Kierkegaard writes:

> He, too, who lives ethically experiences mood, but for him this is not the highest experience; because he has infinitely chosen himself he sees the mood below him. The remainder which will not "go into" mood is precisely the continuity which is to him the highest thing.[27]

Researchers have found that when there is a continuity in one's narrative, in fact, in any good narrative which is character-driven stimulates in the brain the flow of the molecule oxytocin.

When your brain is saturated with this chemical (sometimes called the "love hormone") it feels good and you are likely to become more attached and loyal to those in your community.[28] No wonder somebody living Ethically who can see their whole lives as a continuous story and interprets all the changes of the flat world in that light, is more relaxed, more sociable, more likely to see their lives as a chance to serve others.

In this connection, Kierkegaard adds that Ethical individuals see life as beautiful, even the humdrum activities of the job and the home. How beautiful, for such a person with this point of view sees how all these activities reflect the beauty of the idea that we all are called to work as a duty.[29] The love for your spouse and child is part of what life is supposed to be like. Answering that email, dealing with that customer (even the difficult one) is a reflection of the duty of us all to work. And so these tasks take on a cosmic significance. They are part of the globalized economy which impacts every human being, a contribution to the whole of human well-being. There is a beauty in looking at life in this Ethical point of view. Kierkegaard spoke of it as "expressing the universal-human in individual life."[30]

Being ethical just makes sense when you look at life in light of these ideals. When you think this way you do not think of yourself as better than those you serve or who are less talented than you are. For on these grounds, the lowliest person or thing reflects the beauty of the ideal. Both your work and the existence of others is important.[31] Sounds like the Ethical person would be a great boss in our Team-Management ethos, just a genuine nice guy or gal. And when the profitability of offshoring jobs was suggested the ethical CEO and those in administration would also consider responsibility to the employees. Short-term profits over long-term health of the corporation would not be prioritized as much as has been typical of business in the last decades.

Imagine what would happen in a society filled with Ethical individuals and with political leaders committed to this way of living. We would begin to form societies and adopt laws and policies which aimed to overcome the wage gap, to ensure that social justice for all was truly implemented.

The ethical individual is a good employee or supervisor in a globalized economy for other reasons (though his loyalty and lack of flexibility on certain issues related to taking advantage of colleagues or family members might be a liability in some cases). Kierkegaard notes that to be ethical is to reveal oneself, to become revealed regarding what one wants to become.[32] This is in sharp contrast to the aesthetic individual who is ironic, a person whom you never really know because he or she is always changing with the latest social trend or with what the new boss wants. Given this openness, the ethical individuals are also able to render an account of themselves, are honest in assessing who they are.[33] In a business and educational environment marked by evaluation, is not the ethical individual whom you want on the payroll?

Still more virtues: Kierkegaard notes that being ethical is what teaches you to venture, for you are willing to venture everything for what might be nothing. What is good is not some abstract sense of the good. It is what you make concrete by your life that counts.[34] The ethical individual is the sort of risk-taker who can thrive in a market economy, a doer, not just a thinker.

How about it? Is not the Ethical Way of Life a good alternative to Aesthetic living in our flat world? Is this not a lifestyle that escapes hopelessness and aimlessness while still providing a chance for happiness, a way to living on the peaks even in a flat world? Those of us with a loyalty to our job, who feel loyalty towards those with whom we work, having been loyal to our families and love our communities may also be living this.

THE PEAKS AND VALLEYS OF THE ETHICAL WAY OF LIFE

The Ethical Stage of Life is not only a way of life that can enable you to thrive professionally. There are lots of personal benefits that we've noted which I don't want you to overlook. And in closing, I also don't want you to miss what it fails to provide, the valleys of despair into which living this way can leave us.

The Ethical individual is said by Kierkegaard to grasp himself in his eternal validity and is overwhelmed by its fullness. And this leads to indescribable bliss, a sense of absolute security.[35] We've already noted why this is the case Biologically, as when you engage in realities greater than your narrow interests, the brain secretes the amphetamine-like chemical dopamine which leads to happiness and more energy. You're not bored or empty with this sort of view on life, for now, you understand the purpose of all you do in relation to what is infinite and eternal.

Sex is better when you live Ethically. We've already noted that in addition to the brain chemical dopamine secreted during heterosexual intercourse, in long-term commitments the molecule **oxytocin** is secreted. This chemical is crucial for promoting bonding between mother and child. But guys and women enjoy it as a result of snuggling and in long-term relationships (you don't get it in casual sexual relationships). This molecule makes you feel good, promotes a sense of well-being, and alleviates mental stress. (It may even play a role in promoting spirituality.)[36] See, Ethical living is not just good for your behavior and your happiness. It makes sex better. Life is better in the flat world, when you lead it Ethically, it seems.

I don't want to stop here with the impression given that all is well in the flat world with an Ethical style of life, that there are nothing but peaks associated with this style of life. Kierkegaard would not let me. We need to examine the valleys.

Besides the problems living at the Ethical Stage can create professionally because of the perception that individuals living this way are "goodie-two-shoes," not sufficiently flexible, even too full of themselves, the perfectionism associated with those seeking to live ethically can readily put us in the valley. When you have high ideals, a vision of high standards, and a commitment really to living that way, failure is always on the horizon. As honest with themselves as ethical people are thought to be, it is not surprising that they are always struggling with despair. And then finite as we are, we are led to despair over our finite inability to grasp or embody the infinite.[37] Melancholy is innate in the human condition, and the Ethical individual must always struggle with it.[38] Kierkegaard calls this the "sickness unto death," and there is no escape. He writes:

> Just as the physician might say that there lives perhaps not one single man who is in perfect health, so one might say perhaps that there lives not one single man who after all is not to some extent in despair... At any rate there has lived no one outside of Christendom who is not in despair, and no one in Christendom, unless he be a true Christian, and if he is not quite that, he is somewhat in despair after all.[39]

The introduction of Christianity here is timely and deliberate on Kierkegaard's and my part. Ethical people are ready to hear all this Christian talk about sin and need for a Savior. Unlike the Aesthetic individual who could care less about ideals, the Ethical individual lives a life shaped by these ideals. And too often his or her action falls short, as we lose ourselves by doing the world's thing (following the latest mood or trend). No matter how hard I may try to do my duty, it is never fully realized. Clearly my finiteness falls short of the infinite, is not grounded in the infinite and its ever-expanding possibilities.[40] This awareness gets us ready to hear about God.

But as Kierkegaard notes, "Against God we are always wrong."[41]

No way out of the despair, the sickness, it seems, for the ethical individual. The effort to live out one's duty, to find infinite meaning in a meaningless world, seems ultimately doomed to unhappiness and failure. And the scepter of death and its uncertainty is always in the background.[42] Readers who have tried to maintain integrity and loyalty in the flat world, have you not felt these feelings? And if you've been following the latest moods and trends, you're not any happier than the Ethical types, are you? Kierkegaard offers a summary that explains a possible way out, by pointing out the ultimate failure to which an Ethical way of life leads:

> ... the particular individual is the individual who has his *telos* [end] in the universal, and his ethical task is to express himself constantly in it, to abolish his particularity in order to become the universal. As soon as the individual would assert himself and his particularity over against the universal he sins, and only by recognizing this can he again reconcile himself with the universal... and he can labor himself out of this only by penitently abandoning himself as the particular in the universal.[43]

But because of the sickness unto death, we cannot lose ourselves in the universal, totally embody the universal moral principles. Besides, to lose ourselves in a morality to which we do not feel committed would entail suicide, a loss of our particularity. Is that what the ethical way of life leads us to – either to end your particularity by means of suicide, drift back into an Aesthetic lifestyle in which we lose ourselves, or to live as a failure? The only way out, the way to find happiness, it seems, is the life of faith which overturns the relationship between the universal and the particular which traps people who try to live ethically.[44] Want to take that leap with me and Kierkegaard? From the valley in which we find ourselves, religious life can find us some peaks.

NOTES

1. Richard Sennett, The Corrosion of Character: The Personal Consequences of Work in the New Capitalism (New York and London: W. W. Norton, 1998), p.91.

2. Søren Kierkegaard, Concluding Unscientific Postscript, trans. David Swenson and Walter Lowrie (Princeton, NJ: Princeton University Press, 1941), p.288.

3. Søren Kierkegaard, Either/Or, Vol.II, trans Walter Lowrie (Princeton, NJ: Princeton University Press, 1944), pp.234-235; Kierkegaard, Concluding Unscientific Postscript, pp.115ff. (esp. p.142).

4. Kierkegaard, Either/Or, Vol.II, p.226.

5. Kierkegaard, Concluding Unscientific Postscript, pp.280,291.

6. Kierkegaard, Either/Or, Vol.II, p. 257.

7. Ibid., pp.256-257.

8. Ibid., Vol.I, p.167.

9. Daniel G. Amen, Change Your Brain, Change Your Life (New York: Three Rivers Press, 1998), esp. p.116.

10. Meg Brenan, "Americans Say U.S. Moral Values Not Good and Getting Worse," at https://news.gallup.com/poll/257954/americans-say-moral-values-not-good-getting-worse..., accessed April 20,2020.

11. Pew Research Center, Where Americans Find Meaning in Life, at https:www/pewforum.org/2018/11/20/where-americans-find-meaning-om-life/, accessed April 20, 2020.

12. Kierkegaard, Either/Or, Vol.II, p.267.

13. Ibid., p.299.

14. Ibid., p.292.

15. Thomas L. Friedman, The World Is Flat: A Brief History of the Twenty-First Century (paperback ed.; New York: Pacidor/Farrar, Straus and Giroux, 2007), esp. pp.339.

16. Nicholas Eberstadt, America's Invisible Crisis: Men Without Work (West Conshohocken, PA: Templeton Press, 2016); Jean Twenge, iGen: Why Today's Super-Connected Kids Are Growing Up Less Rebellious, More Tolerant, Less Happy – and Completely Unprepared for Adulthood (New York and London: Simon & Schuster, 2017), esp. pp.182-183.

17. Kierkegaard, Either/Or, Vol.II, p.234.

18. Ibid., pp.296-297.

19. Ibid.

20. Ibid., p.298.

21. Alan Jasanoff, The Biological Mind (New York: Basic Books, 2018), p.168; Andrew Newberg and Mark Robert Waldman, Why We Believe What We Believe (New York and London: Fee Press, 2006), pp.232ff.

22. David Brinn, "Israeli researchers discover gene for altruism," in Our Jerusalem, posted January 23, 2005, at http://www.ourjerusalem.com/news/story/news2005124html, accessed December 28. 2007, reporting on research by Richard Ebstein, Modern Psychiatry (January 2005).

23. Kierkegaard, Either/Or, Vol.II, p.234.

24. Kierkegaard, Concluding Unscientific Postscript, p.390.

25. Kierkegaard, Either/Or, Vol.II, p.301.

26. Ibid., p.234.

27. Ibid.

28. Paul J. Zak, "Why Your Brain Loves Good Storytelling," <u>Harvard Business Review</u>, October 28, 2014, at https://hbr.org/2014/10/why-you-brain-loves-good-storytelling, accessed April 24, 20202; Marcelo Ceberio, " Trust, Generosity, Affection: The Benefits of Oxytocin," <u>Exploring Your Mind</u>, December 4, 2019, at
https://exploringyourmind.com/trust-generosity-affection-the-benefits-of-oxytocin, accessed April 24, 2020.

29. Kierkegaard, <u>Either/Or</u>, Vol.II, p.289.

30. <u>Ibid</u>., p.333.

31. <u>Ibid</u>., pp.289,328-329.

32. <u>Ibid</u>., pp.265,327.

33. <u>Ibid</u>., pp.265.

34. Kierkegaard, <u>Concluding Unscientific Postscript</u>, pp.133,138.

35. Kierkegaard, <u>Either/Or</u>, Vol.II, pp.235-236.

36. Amen, pp.86-87.

37. Kierkegaard, <u>Either/Or</u>, Vol.II, pp.212-214,222-223,224,225-226.

38. <u>Ibid</u>., p.293.

39. Søren Kierkegaard, <u>Fear and Trembling and The Sickness Unto Death</u>, trans. Walter Lowrie (Princeton, NJ: Princeton University Press, 1941), p.155.

40. <u>Ibid</u>., p.163.

41. Kierkegaard, <u>Either/Or</u>, Vol.II, p.354.

42. Kierkegaard, <u>Concluding Unscientific Postscript</u>, pp.147ff.

43. Kierkegaard, <u>Fear and Trembling and The Sickness Unto Death</u>, pp.64-65.

44. <u>Ibid</u>., pp.65,66.

Chapter 6

RELIGIOUS LIFE: FROM THE SHALLOWS TO THE MOUNTAIN-TOP

If you've taken seriously the kind of despair that will transpire when you try to live Ethically in the flat world, recognizing the bankruptcy of living Aesthetically for the moment and the latest passion or mood, when you're really convinced that there's nowhere else to go, you might finally be ready to take this leap. The idea that religious commitment might "save your soul," give you sanity to face tomorrow in our fast-paced, no-commitment world, seems so naïve, so politically incorrect. But that is just the point of Religious living, why it is such a good way to live in our flat world. The Religious individual frankly "doesn't give a damn" about what "sophisticated," globalized denizens of the flat world and their media tell us. The Religious individual, someone who lives a healthy, happy life in our flat world, knows that the secret of life is self-consciously to live on the edge – to live in the peaks of valleys of life. Want to join me and Kierkegaard in learning how it can happen?

Remember, it begins with taking ownership of who you are, what Kierkegaard calls subjectivity or inwardness. He says that such subjectivity, taking responsibility for who you are and the quality of your own life, is truth.[1] In fact, it is the highest good, when you concentrate on yourself in relation to the infinite. And it's the Infinite we want; we want to get our day-to-day duties in dialogue with eternal patterns in order to make our mundane (dare I say seemingly boring activities) meaningful. That's what Ethical people try to do – imperfectly as we came to recognize in the last chapter. Christianity, because of its unique and surprising paradoxical teachings, is best able to stimulate this sort of subjectivity.[2] He writes:

> Subjectivity is the truth. By virtue of the relationship subsisting between the eternal truth and the existing individual, the paradox came into being. Let us now go further, let us suppose that the eternal essential truth is itself a paradox. How does the paradox come into being? By putting the eternal essential truth into juxtaposition with existence. Hence when we posit such a conjunction with the truth itself, the truth

becomes a paradox. The eternal truth has come into being in time; this is the paradox.[3]

What makes Christianity the highest form of subjectivity? In these comments, Kierkegaard hints at the answer. There is something about the Christian faith which makes it paradoxical. In this quotation, the Danish forerunner of Existentialism contends that Christianity makes the audacious claim that the eternal truth (God) has come in time (in the first century in the Man Jesus). In fact, he even claims that the idea that God became man is so rationally absurd that it could never have entered into a human being's mind naturally. Christ is the Absolute Paradox.[4] The divinity of the Man Jesus is a contradiction of all that is rational.

Kierkegaard proceeded to name other paradoxes – other Christian commitments designed to blow our minds and lead the cultural elite among us to shake their heads and wonder about those naïve, credulous Christians. Of course, we all know how socially incorrect Christianity is in the eyes of the social gurus. As early as the 1990s the Yale Law School professor Stephen Carter was observing how in educated and public policy circles as well as in the media, the views of religious leaders are regarded as sectarian, even as a kind of fanaticism.[5] Kierkegaard wants followers of Jesus to own that image, rather than to be embarrassed about it, to stick the middle finger at such critics with all the paradoxical beliefs of Christian faith. With that attitude, the faithful will even become more subjective and inward, less likely to get caught up in the latest passions and moods of the economic sphere.

Who in their right mind can believe the audacious Christian claim that the historical events like the ones in which Jesus was engaged could provide eternal happiness? Kierkegaard put it this way:

> If the contradiction is this: to base an eternal happiness upon the relation to something historical – then this contradiction is not resolved by this consideration that the historical fact in question is constituted out of a contradiction, when nevertheless one is to hold fast that it is historical; and if this is not to be held fast, then indeed the eternal has not become historical.[6]

Note here again, a point which we previously observed, that Kierkegaard seems to promise that becoming religious (in a Christian way) can lead to eternal happiness. Christian living can offer the kind of mountain-top experience we cannot find living in the flat world Aesthetically or even Ethically! But it happens only through Christ and with Him the awareness of the impossible possibility that an eternal gift has been given through ordinary, contingent historical means. This is another logical contradiction which entails the need for those wanting to live as Christians to totally invest themselves in these beliefs. And there are more instances of these paradoxes of faith.

There is the lowliness of Jesus Christ for one item, His ordinariness is certainly not befitting One Who is the King.[7] The fact that He suffered is a further cause of offense.[8] Another cause for offense in Jesus and His Message relates to His engagement with the established order. As He offended the establishment of His day, so Jesus is likely to be offensive to today's globalized, establishment, an order based on "go with the flow and stand for nothing."[9]

Though Kierkegaard does not make this point as explicit, it is consistent with his thinking to observe how offensive to reason it is to note that "God's love is greater than our love," that despite our ultimate failure of our efforts to live Ethically, our despair, and sickness unto death, yet He loves us still.[10] Indeed, with this insight that Christ has died for us, 'the doubt of the forgiveness of sins [is] impossible," Kierkegaard says.[11] Reason cannot bear this insight. It is downright offensive to our ordinary ways of thinking about ourselves and others, perverted as they are!

Earlier I called your attention to the eternal happiness which Kierkegaard promises those of us in the flat world, even in the midst of our despair. Neurobiology provides some authorization for these findings and explains how the paradoxes of faith assist this happiness (though I am by no means certain that the Danish loner would approve of these points). It was also previously noted that in many higher human activities the front part of the human bring (the prefrontal cortex) is activated. And as a result, the brain is flooded by two pleasurable neurochemicals – dopamine which facilitates the formation of new neural connections and also energizes us and oxytocin which stimulates nurturing feelings. It seems that both of these neurochemicals are secreted in spiritual/religious experience.[12]

These scholars have also found that in such experiences, the back part of our brain (the parietal lobe) shuts down. This is the part of our brain that orients us in time and space. In the deepest spiritual experiences, you lose yourself. This is where the reason-confounding paradoxes of Kierkegaard play a role. When faith is presented in ways that confound our reason and the truisms of the culture, then we are more likely to get all wrapped up in the truths of Christian faith, in the realities that are portrayed. On the other hand, were Christianity presented more as making sense, linking with our present experience, the back part of our brains would be less likely to shut down. Indeed, then Christian thinking would reinforce our existing worldview, our sense of space and time.

Get the point? The best way to stimulate spirituality may be with Kierkegaard's (Lutheran) paradoxes confounding reason. The great Danish thinker has other ways of making this point, ways of getting us to shut down our parietal lobes. So intent he is on having Christians focused only on the things of faith, on subjectivity and not what surrounds them, that he insists that there can be no disciples at second hand. We've already alluded to this commitment on Kierkegaard's part, but let's delve into it in more detail. Reason teaches us that what is differentiated by time is not absolute, the great Danish thinker notes. And yet Christians believe that the absolute fact is historical. There is only one possible resolution, Kierkegaard notes:

> ... Now just as the historical gives occasion for the contemporary to become a disciple, but only it must be noted through receiving the condition from God Himself, since otherwise we speak Socratically, so the testimony of contemporaries gives occasion for each successor to become a disciple but only it must be noted through receiving the condition from the God Himself.[13]

The disciple of Jesus, contemporary with Him, loses oneself and one's circumstances, is caught up in Jesus' life and the experience of His contemporaries. The role of the parietal lobe in downgraded when you get caught up in a narrative. You lose yourself. And the latest Neurobiological research indicates that when you are caught up in a narrative that renders its characters to you in a contemporaneous manner, the process is facilitated by the release of the good-feeling rain chemical oxytocin.[14] Again, it is evident how when we live the Christian life as Kierkegaard prescribes, happiness is likely to follow.

GETTING REALISTIC ABOUT LIVING RELIGIOUSLY IN A FLAT WORLD

There are other ways in which Kierkegaard introduces paradoxes and offenses into his vision of Religious life. It is important that we note these additional observations, lest we become too unrealistic about the Religious Stage of Life, opt for it for Aesthetic reasons (because it might feel good or be beneficial to us).

For one item, we must note that not everything about becoming a Christian is joyful. Kierkegaard notes that as Christ suffered, so will Christians:

> Thou wilt bear in mind that if there is to be any seriousness in stationing oneself or standing besides the Cross, it must be in the situation of contemporaneousness, where it will mean *actually* to incur suffering with Him...[15]

Indeed there is no eternal happiness without suffering and its decisive expression is guilt.[16]

Why not? Why is this realism about ourselves so essential for the experience of eternal happiness? For the same reason that we must grapple with the paradoxes and rational absurdities of the Christian faith. These risks and sense of logical dead-ends heighten our subjectivity and inwardness to the highest levels of intensity.[17] And as we've noted, it is precisely when we are subjective in our faith that the faithful will truly live out the Christian life, seek to become Christian. And with that experience and style of life, the Neurobiologists say, comes happiness (all the dopamine and oxytocin secreted in our brains). Kierkegaard says much the same. When we put aside all that is external, do not let what is going on in the world and around us determine who we are, we experience eternal happiness:

> But in his relation to an eternal happiness the individual has to do solely with himself in inwardness... In his outward life the idea of an eternal happiness will not *profit* him at all, since the idea is not actually present to him until he has learned to despise the external and to forget the earthly mind's notion of what is profitable.[18]

No wonder the experience of putting everything external aside, becoming more subjective, would lead to eternal happiness. Our Danish guide to these matters notes that the meaning of life is ours when in subjectivity we human beings realize that life is all about knowing God:

> For the knowledge of God is the most decisive factor in every human life, and without this knowledge, a man would become absolutely nothing. Without God he would perhaps scarcely be able to grasp the most elementary secret of the truth, that he is of himself absolutely nothing; even less would he be able to understand it is his need of God that constitutes his highest perfection.[19]

Further commenting on eternal happiness, Kierkegaard goes on to say that there is a great cost for this happiness, a kind of madness towards the things of the world, but great security.[20] An awareness of sin and renunciation of the things of the world is paradoxically related to eternal happiness. If you just keep your life flat in the flat world, haven't descended into the valley of despair and sin-consciousness, you may miss the mountain top. We globalized citizens aren't as good and as well-adjusted as we think we are. We need this insight, Kierkegaard adds, for "I will not build my eternal happiness on any deed I may have done... since I can still do nothing of myself..."[21] Liberated by our total dependence on God, Kierkegaard notes that one living religiously will also enjoy some laughs, see humor in life, when they reflect on their sin, suffering, and all the despair experienced in daily life. Kierkegaard observes that humor involves putting our guilt or tragedy in relation to an eternal happiness. In that comparison, the guilt is "less than nothing." There is comedy in that the religious individual is no different from anyone else.[22] Have a good time, have fun in the flat world. It's not so serious after all.

OTHER CHARACTERISTICS OF THE RELIGIOUS LIFE

The Religious Stage of Living includes as few other characteristics which are relevant for lie in the flat world. One of these Kierkegaard calls the *Teleological Suspension of the Ethical*, a commitment in line with Pauline themes (Galatians 5:1-6). In order to leap from the Ethical Stage to the Religious, commitment to a Law-oriented Ethic must be suspended. This is the "infinite resignation of faith" Kierkegaard claims.[23] It is a willingness to renounce everything temporal for the sake of the eternal. It is absurd (another paradox). Kierkegaard uses the story of Abraham's willingness to sacrifice Isaac in response to God's command (Genesis 22).[24] For Abraham was ready to break the Commandment "Thou shall not kill" on the Lord's demand.

Kierkegaard explains what is at stake in this commitment. He speaks of the individual asserting himself in his particularity over against the universal. If the highest thing that can be said of a human being is that he or she must abandon himself/herself in the universal, then the Ethical has become the source of eternal blessing, and not God. But faith says paradoxically that this is not the case, "that the particular is higher than the universal."[25] Thus the Teleological Suspension of the Ethical is about absolute duty to God, making clear that God and not the Ethical principle is the infinite source of all.[26] There is a comedy, Kierkegaard notes, in the absurdity of religious people holding themselves to the Ethical, but you can only see that from the perspective of suspending the Ethical in the name of Religion.[27]

Should we look for children to sacrifice, break all the rules? No, only when God directs it. But individuals living religiously (seeking to become Christian) are risk-takers, not bound by the old values or ways of doing things. Indeed, like Jesus they live incognito, like everyone else, just as God is hidden to modern life.[28] Christians who take Kierkegaard's advice are not holy-rollers, and their willingness to suspend ethical norms will not be done ostentatiously.

Another feature of the religious life on Kierkegaard's grounds is that Christians don't get bored easily. Every minute counts, because the moment is filled with eternity.[29] Things are urgent. There is no time to waste. These characteristics can help the religious individual to thrive and have a lot more fun and fulfillment in the flat world. More on that in the Conclusion.

INSIGHTS ABOUT LIFE IN THE FLAT WORLD

Kierkegaard's analysis of the Religious Stage explains a lot about what is happening in American Christianity today. We don't want to live with these paradoxes. We want an attractive, rationally sensible faith. The academy does Theology that way. Apologetics dominates. The dominant theologies in American mainline seminaries, what is taught to the pastors (esp. but not exclusively by Pastoral Theology Departments), are versions of faith that make sense, that accord with the values of our flat world. But it has not done much good. Kierkegaard said something like this nearly 2 centuries ago. The established church has not changed much:

> But observe what a poor service one renders Christianity by doing away with the possibility of offence and making it an amiable, sentimental paganism... And verily the eighteen centuries, which have not contributed an iota to prove the truth of Christianity, have on the contrary contributed with steadily increasing power to do away with Christianity. It is by no means true, as one might consistently suppose when one acclaims the proof of the eighteen centuries, that now in the nineteenth century people are far more thoroughly convinced of the truth of Christianity than they were in the first and second generations – it is rather true (though it certainly sounds rather like a satire...) that just in proportion as the proof supposedly has increased in cogency... fewer and fewer persons are convinced.[30]

A reasonable, healthy, or politically correct Christianity seems to be what Christianity in the West (esp. in America) has become. Witness how until they received the emperor's (Trump's) permission, and only then, almost all the mainline churches and Evangelicals in bed with the Republican Party made sure that they followed the directives of all the politicians to shut down churches in the name of health during the 2020 pandemic. Faith dare not be in tension with the best medical practices or nurture the faithful in "un-American" unhealthy ways. Until you get the government's or the social gurus' permission, to heck with the First Commandment and honoring the Sabbath. And when you do, how then is Christianity any different from any of the prevailing options of the flat world? And since the faithful are not visibly different, it's hardly surprising that aesthetic people would find little appealing in or not understand what the faithful are talking about or find it rather boring when the faithful try to talk about eternal happiness and infinity.

Is this why we don't have the personal investment in the faith, why mainline Christianity is losing ground. Christianity is just an objective reality for many believers? For many laity, it's the pastor's baby. Or we view faith Aesthetically.

We'll be religious as long as it meets our needs. Of course, nothing (not even Religion) satisfies Aesthetically. And so the mega-churches playing to that audience have succeeded – but only for a while. Kierkegaard's observations in his own context certainly still seem appropriate to ours. He wrote:

> But the modern age has done away with Christ, either by casting Him out and appropriating His teaching, or by making Him fantastic...[31]

Church leaders and theologians in the flat world have a lot to learn from Kierkegaard.

From the Shallows to the Top of the Mountain in a Flat World: Kierkegaard Shows Us the Way

The great Danish thinker teaches us a lot about life in the flat world. If you live aesthetically, as many of us do, one is ruled by passion, and that just leads to a sense of meaninglessness, boredom, and despair. In the ethical life, one is ruled by societal regulations. You can lose yourself, and you never avoid guilt and anxiety. But in a truly religious life, total faith in God reigns. Of course, one can never be truly free, and this still leads to boredom, anxiety, and despair. True faith doesn't lead to freedom, but it relieves the Psychological effects of human existence. Kierkegaard claims that the only way to make life worthwhile is to embrace faith in God, and that faith necessarily involves embracing the absurd. However, as we've noted, living that way seems to shut down your parietal lobe in the brain, helps you lose yourself, get totally dependent on God, and then you get the good-feeling and healthy brain chemicals saturating your brain. It all leads to happiness and good humor, to the mountain-tops of life. But you need to experience the lows along with it all. Religious life keeps the shallows in the flat world along with the mountain tops.

It's not that you absent yourself from life, then, or stop making contributions to the flat world. It's just that you don't let those business and professional dynamics or the media message, not even moral commitments, determine who you are. This what it means to say that the Religious existence is incognito. Only such a lifestyle, engaged "in" the dynamics of flexibility and self-concern necessary to cope with economic realities, but not "of" these dynamics in the sense of not ultimately being defined by them, can find joy and true fulfillment.

We need a sense, like Kierkegaard teaches us, that not everything in life is about making a profit or meeting one's needs. Some moments in life have eternal significance, and we won't want to miss them! Let's close by examining exactly how this can be the way you live in our flat world, what it looks like concretely, and where or how you might find the peaks and the valleys.

But at this point and in closing, let's not forget another very important point Kierkegaard makes. We need to remember that we can't make ourselves religious, make ourselves aware of sin, or even truly become subjective. Subjectivity gets us to the mountaintop when we are totally subjected to the infinite, renounce everything for the sake of the eternal. This is the paradox of how in asserting ourselves we lose the self. We are transformed by Christ. Without Him, we are not even aware of our sin.[32] Kierkegaard goes so far as to claim that Christ provides the conditions for understanding and faith.[33] It is grace that brings this about, transforming the Christian life into "sheer gentleness, grace, lovingkindness, and compassion."[34] This stress on what God does and not what we do accords with the Neurobiological dynamics we have noted. If you think you are doing the heavy lifting in spirituality, your focus on the One Who is not you is diminished, and so you are more likely to occupy yourself with immediate task, activate your parietal lobe at the cost of losing yourself and your focus on the One Who is greater than you are. There are costs in these experiences, losing the focus on God and returning to the anxieties of ethical and aesthetic lifestyles. Let's now try to picture how we can live this way and what it looks like in our flat, interconnected world.

NOTES

1. Søren Kierkegaard, Concluding Unscientific Postscript, trans. David Swenson and Walter Lowrie (Princeton, NJ: Princeton University Press, 1941), pp.248,127.

2. Ibid.

3. Ibid. p.187.

4. Søren Kierkegaard, Philosophical Fragments, trans. David Swenson (Princeton, NJ: Princeton University Press, 1967), p.44; Søren Kierkegaard, Training In Christianity, trans. Walter Lowrie (Princeton, NJ: Princeton University Press, 1967), p.128.

5. Stephen Carter, The Culture of Disbelief: How American Law and Politics Trivialize Religious Devotion (New York: Basic Books, 1993), p.23.

6. Kierkegaard, Concluding Unscientific Postscript, p.513.

7. Søren Kierkegaard, Training In Christianity, trans. Walter Lowrie (Princeton, NJ: Princeton University Press, 1941), p.108.

8. Ibid., p.136.

9. Ibid., pp.87ff.

10. Søren Kierkegaard, Either/Or, Vol.II, trans Walter Lowrie (Princeton, NJ: Princeton University Press, 1944), p.355; Kierkegaard, Edifying Discourses, in Training In Christianity, p.271.

11. Søren Kierkegaard, Edifying Discourses, in Training In Christianity, p.271.

12. Andrew Newberg and Mark R. Waldman, Why We Believe What We Believe (New York: Free Press, 2006); Andrew Newberg and Mark R. Waldman, How God Changes Your Brain (New York: Ballantine, 2010), pp.55-56; Andrew Newberg and J. Iversen, "The neural basis of the complex mental task of meditation: neurotransmitter and neurochemical considerations," Medical Hypotheses 61, No.2 (2003): 288; Daniel Amen, Change Your Brain, Change Your Life (New York: Three Rivers Press, 1998), p.93; Patty Van Capellen, Baldwin Way, Suzannah Isgett, and Barbara Fredrickson, "Effects of oxytocin administration on spirituality and emotional responses to meditation," Social Cognitive and Affective Neuroscience Oct. 11 (10), 2016: 1579-1587.

13. Kierkegaard, Philosophical Fragments, pp.125-126.

14. Paul Zak, "Why our Brain Loves Good Storytelling," Harvard Business Review (Oct. 218, 2014).

15. Kierkegaard, Training In Christianity, p.171.

16. Kierkegaard, Concluding Unscientific Postscript, pp.386ff.,468ff.

17. Ibid., p.494; Kierkegaard, Training In Christianity, pp.83ff.

18. Kierkegaard, Concluding Unscientific Postscript, p.346.

19. Søren Kierkegaard, "Man's Need of God Constitutes His Highest Perfection," in Edifying Discourses: A Selection, ed. Paul Holmer, trans. David Swenson and Lillian Swenson (New York and London: Harper & Row, 1958), p.176.

20. Kierkegaard, Concluding Unscientific Postscript, p.346.

21. Søren Kierkegaard, "The Expectation of an Eternal Happiness," in Edifying Discourses: A Selection, p.135.

22. Kierkegaard, Concluding Unscientific Postscript, pp.492-494,464-465.

23. Søren Kierkegaard, Fear and Trembling and The Sickness Unto Death, trans. Walter Lowrie (Princeton, NJ: Princeton University Press, 1941), pp.59-60.

24. Ibid., pp.27ff.

25. Ibid., pp.64-65.

26. Ibid., p.91.

27. Kierkegaard, Concluding Unscientific Postscript, pp.464-465.

28. Kierkegaard, Training In Christianity, p.127.

29. Søren Kierkegaard, "Our Duty To Remain in the Debt of Love to One Another," Works of Love, trans. David Swenson and Lillian Marvin Swenson (Princeton, N.J.: Princeton University Press, 1946), p.148; Kierkegaard, Concluding Unscientific Postscript, pp.512-513.

30. Kierkegaard, Training In Christianity, pp.143-144.

31. Ibid., p.127.

32. Kierkegaard, Philosophical Fragments, p.19.

33. Ibid., pp.17-18.

34, Kierkegaard, Training In Christianity, p.71.

CONCLUSION

Kierkegaard gives a sound summary of the transition from how most of us are living in the flat world to the peaks and valleys of faith. He wrote:

> Man lives undisturbed in a self-centered life, until there awakens with him the paradox of self-love, in the form of love for another, the object of his longing... The lover is so completely transformed by the paradox of love that he scarcely recognizes himself... [1]

> In like manner, the paradoxical passion of Reason, while as yet a mere presentiment, retroactively affects man and his self-knowledge, so that he who thought to know himself is no longer certain whether his is a more strangely composite animal... or if perchance his nature contains a gentler divine part... But what is this unknown something with which the Reason collides when inspired by its paradoxical passion, with the result of unsettling even man's knowledge of himself? It is the Unknown... So let us call this unknown *the God*.[2]

Kierkegaard knows us 21st-century citizens of the globalized interconnected world so well. Self-centered we are, always looking for the latest fad or new thing, always on the run, seeking what's good for us (on the job, in relationships, even if we're engaged in community or spiritual matters). We'll live that way pretty much undisturbed until we realize how unhappy (full of despair) we are. Then we might be ready to take a leap and try to love ourselves enough to take stock and jump into relationships in which loving others is more important than self-centerdness.

Take a self-assessment on how you're living. Think about these questions:

ARE YOU LIVING AESTHETICALLY?

1. Why are you working? To make a living?

2. Why do you stay in the relationships you have? Because they meet your needs?

3. If you are with people and you get a text message, what do you do? At least read and maybe even answer the latest text?

4.   How important is it that you get the higher salary, the bigger house, the latest must-have item? Do you want other people you know to notice what you have, even to envy you?

5.   Are you moody?

6.   Are you bored a lot of times, want to be entertained?

7.   Do you know where you're headed in life, who you are, and what your life stands for in the grand scheme of things?

Answered "yes" to a lot of the final questions in a series of questions on the first four points as well as to #5 and #6 and "no" to the question in #7, then ask yourself some more questions: Are you really happy? Sick of the need to keep reinventing yourself in order to succeed or have peace to the point that you've lost a sense of how to live and of who you are? Then you might be living aesthetically. On the other hand, if you answered "no" to the last/only questions in the first five clusters above and "yes" to the last question, then maybe when I turn to the next set of questions, you'll find yourself. First, though, let's get back to our readers who might be living aesthetically and want to take a leap, to turn things around.

Take a Leap

Let's assume you're not happy in short-term, flexibility living that we've just been describing. You've already taken the first step Kierkegaard advises, when you've examined yourself inwardly and become subjective. This is a kind of self-love or self-concern. Kierkegaard predicts that you will not just be focused on your own well being when you undertake these processes. If you just stop with yourself, with feeling good, then you're still living aesthetically. OK, take the leap. Let's try to assess if you've made it.

ARE YOU LIVING ETHICALLY?

1.   Why are you working? Because it's the right thing to do and it's your duty?

2.   Why do you stay in the relationships you have? Because you care about those people, understand yourself to be responsible about their welfare, and feel loyal to the company and its people?

3.   What are the most important things in life? Family, friends, community, being good to others?

4. When you are with friends or family and you get a text message on your phone, what do you do? Ignore the text and keep the conversation going with the most important people in your life?

5. Do you try to live according to some moral standards?

6. Do you hang in there when things get tough?

7. Do you know who you are and what you want to do with the rest of your life? Be sure that mission is bigger than you are, has to do with making a contribution to others (and the bigger that dream the better).

Answered "yes" to a lot of the final questions in each of these clusters of questions? Chances are you are living ethically, or at least trying to. There's more satisfaction in life, more peaks in life when you live this way, Kierkegaard says. But then there are also more self-conscious valleys too.

But are you? How are you doing on living up to the values you've chosen for yourself? St. Paul (Romans 7:7-23) and Kierkegaard say you are probably flunking. I am too. Maybe sometimes you have just punted on these commitments, lived more aesthetically. Abandoning an ethical way of life for the Aesthetic Style of Living is not uncommon, and each time you need to repent self-consciously if you ever return to the Ethical Style. But be honest: Aren't you really a failure in all high ideals? If not, if you haven't felt the sickness unto death and a lot of guilt you're kidding yourself. And when you do that, you'll be back to the flat, unexamined way of life of someone living the Aesthetic Style of Life.

If you've really been ethically you realize that your failures are a betrayal of what is best in the life, of its meaning and purpose, of what is bigger than you and me (the Infinite). Feel that way? If not, get more ethical, more devoted to your ideals. Spend more time on the last set of questions (#7) with which you've been grappling (the one about who you are and what you want to do with the rest of your life). Do that with sincerity, and you'll find yourself so low (so sick in your heart) that you might be ready to leap – to leap into the arms of a loving God.

LIVING RELIGIOUSLY

Lots of Americans, Brits, and Western Europeans (not to mention denizens of the Southern Hemisphere) believe in God. But that does not necessarily mean you are living religiously in Kierkegaard's sense. If not, he says (along with a lot of support from brain researchers), don't expect too much happiness and comfort from your faith. Again a few questions to consider:

1. Do you believe and worship because it feels good and you're getting something out of it, for the worship is beautiful?

2. Do you believe because it's the right thing to do, and all your friends are there (or at least believe)?

3. Do you believe because faith is relevant and makes sense?

4. Do you believe like most Americans and Europeans that your faith saves, that God only saves good, well-meaning people?[3]

Answer yes to these questions, and you are not quite ready to become a Christian Kierkegaard's way. Faith may not be having the kind of impact on your life that you would like it too. You may also be enjoying less of that good brain dope (the dopamine and oxytocin) we've already described. You're still pretty flat in the flat world, not found the mountaintop yet.

Yes to the first question entails that your faith is aesthetic. You're doing it because it feels good. (Kierkegaard was very concerned about not mixing the Aesthetic and Religious categories.[4]) Answered yes to the second question, and you have mixed the Religious and the Ethical. (that's probably true if you said "yes" to the last question or if you think your church did the right thing by closing live, in-person worship during the last pandemic and that Christians need to be good Americans or law-abiding citizens everywhere). I'm calling it as I see it.

If you affirmed #3 and believe with a lot of denominational leaders and Religion scholars, then Kierkegaard says you have made religion objective. And a lived faith needs to be subjective. If it's objective, then we can manipulate, believe in a god who is relevant, who gives us what we need or want.[5]

What Becoming Christian Might Look Like for You in a Flat World

With these qualification/warnings in mind, let's review what the religious life would look like for you in a flat, interconnected world. Are you really dissatisfied, not just with aesthetic life (sick of being so flexible that it feels like you've lost yourself sometimes), but also with your own ethical performance? Are you a little scared of what might befall you, your loved ones, your community, and nation, because you've been so out of tune with what life demands, with a sense of eternity? Maybe even unsure of God's judgment? If you don't have those feelings, you're not ready for the religious life, Kierkegaard thinks. Spend a little more time in subjectivity, thinking about life in relation to what is infinite and eternal. You'll eventually get to this awareness of your finiteness, limits, and hypocrisy. The religious life is filled with valleys along with the peaks. It may be tough in the valley, even painful, but you don't get bored like you can in a flat world.

Like we've already noted, hang around Jesus, consider His life and suffering, and all the guilt and anxiety you have felt become sin, the realization that all your self-serving moods and failure to fulfill your duty is a disrespect of the Eternal and Infinite Who stands before you in Christ.[6] Note here, it is not that you by your superior meditative skills and introspection (not even your subjectivity) brought you to experience the true meaning of your despair and anxiety. It all came from god as a result of Christ coming to you.

Focusing on Christ is crucial at this point. But remember it will not happen because you manipulated Christ. It happens because He becomes contemporary with you. Hugh? The whole thing makes no sense. How can this guy who lived over 2000 years ago confront you or me? That's right. Recall the paradoxes considered in the previous chapter. How incredible it is to believe in this Jesus, the absurdity of thinking the finite could bear the infinite, that this Eternal King would suffer. (The belief the God could be Three and still One, that a dead man could rise, or that sick people like us could be spiritually healed, that all in our finite lives should be renounced for God's sake are also absurd.) So don't look for a rational faith, Kierkegaard advises. Realize what a lot of people in the flat world think of Christians, how odd we are.

Kierkegaard wants you to embrace this oddness, not flee it. Realize what a risk you are taking. As he puts it: "To be a Christian has become a thing of naught, mere tomfoolery. "It is a sort of joyful madness.[7] When you have this perspective on faith, it becomes a risk, and so you are likely to take it more seriously. And this focus on your faith, on God, explains the joy that comes with this madness. As we've noted, spiritual experience, concentration on the God and the Infinite, puts the prefrontal cortex of your brain in overdrive with the secretion of pleasurable brain chemicals dopamine and oxytocin secreted. No wonder Christians focused on the risk of faith, on how dependent they are on a God Who doesn't make much sense are so happy. In the valley of absurdity, you'll likely experience the peaks of joy in life.

Continue to reflect on how odd you are in your faith, its nonsensical character, and revel in it. Do everything you can not to get distracted from this perspective and this focus on Christ and the Eternal. Remember that even your Ethical commitments must give way to following Christ (the Teleological Suspension of the Ethical). Sometimes you'll want to surrender everything, even a commitment to morality, in order to follow the Infinite.

What does this way of life look like on a flat, interconnected world? Hints were already given in the previous chapter. The subjective Christian risking it all looks like others on the job, in her or his personal life. The Christian individual is somewhat incognito. But there's something special about those Christians in a flat world. They're odd. Nonconformist. Ready to break all the rules in a quiet, hidden way. They'll make good risk-takers, willing to break the rules and the old traditional ways if it serves the business or their relationships. They're also dutiful and loyal (most of the time) unless they sense a greater calling somewhere else. The job, the community, and their interpersonal relations seem to matter to them. But they're not acting like what happens in their careers (or friendships and personal relations) is the main thing in life or defines them.

They treat most everyone they deal with well, as equals. Even as bosses, they don't act like they're better than anyone else. That surfaces in how rebellious they can be on the job or in their politics. (Recall how these commitments surface in the Ethical Stage for Kierkegaard, that the Religious life is not totally divorced from the Ethical Stage, and that only the ethical individual can understand the paradoxical faith of Christianity.) Also remember that the good-feeling brain chemicals getting pumped in the brains of the faithful both render people more sociable when they saturate our brains. Faith really leads to good works. Most of the time, those trying to become Christians seem happy, at peace with themselves and what's all around them, laugh a lot at the craziness of life, though they have a contemplative side that makes them brooders sometimes.

There's another feature about those Christians. They don't seem to burn out. (Dopamine in greater doses also enhances energy.) Every moment counts for the Christian, because it is the moment of the inbreaking of eternity. Kierkegaard put it this way:

> But to lose the moment is to become immediate... A moment lost, then is the chain of eternity broken; a moment but, then is the continuity of eternity disturbed.[8]

No procrastination for someone becoming Christian. Now is the moment to decide. Further elaborating on the point (sounding much like the forefather of Existentialism), Kierkegaard adds, "For in relation to the absolute there is only one tense: the present." We need to become contemporaneous with Christ.[9] Christians are so focused on the Infinite, because for them, Christ is Present to them in the events of life, much like stories render their characters present to readers.[10] Christ and God are not ideas; they are Persons with whom you interact. Right now they are present for one becoming a Christian!

No wonder those becoming Christian feel they don't have a minute to waste. They're obviously good workers. And since Christ is engaged in every activity, chances are they'll be doing the right (even if controversial) thing, for the neighbor's need, the co-workers' question, or the opportunity to work for justice. And because for those becoming Christian all is done in the presence of Christ, they'll also more likely say "no" to the temptation to break relationships and not put things on the back-burner for the sake of the latest internet post!

The Christian life is certainly one filled with meaning, excitement, and a sense of mission. To be sure, you still taste your lows and descend into the valleys. But the highs and peaks sure beat the flatness of life, the despair so many of us feel. Individuals seeking to become Christian in our flat world have some passions to help make life in a flat world more intense, more committed (to a point), more meaningful, and happier in the midst of all the surface relationships and meandering that life in a globalized, interconnected world seems to entail for many of us. Thank Kierkegaard for the analysis and vision. Only a leap of faith into the loving arms of God can break the monotonous meaninglessness of life in the flat world. Solitary reader, drift no more. For what style of living will you decide? Take some time to think over your choices. But remember, it's urgent to decide and live out your decision.

NOTES

1. Søren Kierkegaard, Philosophical Fragments, trans. David Swenson (Princeton, NJ: Princeton University Press, 1967), p.48.

2. Ibid., pp.48-49.

3. Pew Research Center, "U.S. Protestants Are Not Defined by Reformation-Era Controversies 500 Years Later," (2017); Barna Research Center, "Annual Tracking Study" (2007), barna.com/reserach/barnas-annual-tracking-study-should-americans-stay-spiritually-active-biblical-views-wane, accessed September 29, 2020. In view of the large number of religiously unaffiliated believers in God in Western Europe and the UK it is likely that a vast majority in these nations find salvation to be something we do.

4. Søren Kierkegaard, The Point of View for My Work as An Author: A Report to History, trans. Walter Lowrie (New York, Evanston, and London: Harper & Row, 1962), esp. p.25.

5. For more detailed analysis of this Theology which prevails among the Western intelligentsia and in the mainline denominations, see my Ever Hear of Feuerbach? That's How Come the American and European Church Is In Such a Funk (Portland OR: Cascade, 2020).

6. Kierkegaard, Philosophical Fragments, esp.p.58.

7. Søren Kierkegaard, Training In Christianity, trans. Walter Lowrie (Princeton, NJ: Princeton University Press, 1967), p.71.

8. Søren Kierkegaard, "Our Duty To Remain in the Debt of Love to One Another," Works of Love trans. David Swenson and William M. Swenson (Princeton, NJ: Princeton University Press, 1946), p.148.

9. Kierkegaard, Training In Christianity, p.67.

10. These commitments reflect in the Biblical Narrative Theology of today, in much of the preaching of the Black church, and in Neo-Orthodox Theology. See Martin Luther King, Jr., "I See the Promised Land" (1968), in A Testament of Hope: The Essential Writings of Martin Luther King, Jr., ed. James Washington (San Francisco: Harper & Row, 1986), p.279; Hans Frei, The Eclipse of Biblical Narrative (New Haven, CT and London: Yale University Press, 1974), esp. p.3; Karl Barth, Church Dogmatics, Vol.I/1, trans. G. T. Thompson (Edinburgh: T. & T. Clark, 1936), p.134.

BIBLIOGRAPHY

Amen, Daniel. Change Your Brain, Change Your Life. New York: Three Rivers Press, 1998.

Barna Research Center. "Annual Tracking Study" (2007), barna.com/reserach/barnas-annual-tracking-study-should-americans-stay-spiritually-active-biblical-views-wane. Accessed September 29, 2020.

Barth, Karl. Church Dogmatics, Vol.I/1. Translated by G. T. Thompson. Edinburgh: T & T Clark, 1936.

Brenan, Meg. "Americans Say U.S. Moral Values Not Good and Getting Worse," https"//news.gallup.com/poll/257954/Americans-say-moral-values-not-good-getting-worse... Accessed April 20,2020.

Brinn, David. "Israeli researchers discover gene for altruism," Our Jerusalem (January 23, 2005), https:www,ourjerusalem,com/news/story/news2005124html. Accessed December 28, 2007.

Capellen, Patty Van, Way, Baldwin, Suzannah Isgett, and Barbara Fredrickson. "Effects of O xytocin administration and emotional responses to mediation," Social Cognitive and Affective Neuroscience, (Oct.11 [10], 2016): 1579-1587.

Carr, Nicholas. The Shallows: What the Internet Is Doing To Our Brains. New York and London: W. W. Norton, 2010.

Carter, Stephen. The Culture of Disbelief: How American Law and Politics Trivialize Religious Devotion. New York: Basic Books, 1993.

Ceberoio, Marcelo. "Trust, Generosity, Affection: The Benefits of Oxytocin," Exploring Your Mind (December 4, 2019), https://exporingyourmind.com/trust-generosity-affection-the-benefits-of-oxytocin [accessed April 24, 2020].

Cera, Nicoletta, Ezeio DiPeirro, Francesco Gambi, et al. "The role of the left superior parietal lobe in male sexual behavior: dynamics of distinct components revealed by FMRI," The Journal of Sexual Medicine (June 9, 2012): 1602-1612.

Chakravarty, Ambar. "The neural circuity of visual artistic production and appreciation: A proposition," Annals of Indian Academy of Neurology 15, no.2 (April-June, 2012): 71-75.

Eberstadt, Nicholas. America's Invisible Crisis: Men Without Work. West Conshohocken, PA: Templeton Press, 2016.

Ellingsen, Mark. Ever Hear of Feuerbach? That's How Come the American and European Church Is In Such a Funk. Portland, OR: Cascade, 2020.

Frei, Hans. The Eclipse of Biblical Narrative. New Haven, CT and London: Yale University Press, 1974.

Friedman, Thomas L. The World Is Flat: A Brief History of the Twenty-First Century. paperback ed. New York: Pacidor/Farrar, Straus and Giroux, 2007.

Gallup Poll. 2019 Global Emotions Poll at
www.gallup.com/analytics/248906/gallup-global--emotions-report-2019.
asp [accessed April 20,2020]

Graeber, David. Bull Shit Jobs. New York and London: Simon & Schuster, 2018.

Hamer, Dean. The God Gene: How Faith Is Hardwired Into Our Genes. New
York: Anchor Books, 2004.

Harris Poll. "Here's How Happy Americans Are Right Now,"
theharrispoll.com>heres-how-happy-americans-are-right-now
[accessed March 2, 2020].

Jasanoff, Alan. The Biological Mind. New York: Basic Books, 2018.

Johnson, Steven. "Emotions and the Brain: Love," Discover Magazine, May 1,
2003, http://discovermagazine.com/2003/may/featlove.

Kandel, Eric. In Search of Memory; The Formation of a New Science of the
Mind. New York: Norton, 2006.

Kierkegaard, Søren. Concluding Unscientific Postscript. Translated by David F.
Swenson and Walter Lowrie. Princeton, N. J.: Princeton University Press, 1941.

———. Edifying Discourses: A Selection. Edited by Paul Holmer. New York,
Evanston, and London: Harper & Row, 1958.

———. Either/Or, Vol.I. Translated by David F. Swenson and Lillian M.
Swenson. Princeton, N. J.: Princeton University Press, 1944.

———. Either/Or, Vol.I1. Translated by Walter Lowrie. Princeton, N. J.:
Princeton University Press, 1944.

———. Fear and Trembling and The Sickness Unto Death. Translated by Walter
Lowerie. Princeton, NJ: Princeton University Press, 1941.

———. Papirer. 16 vols. Edited by Peter A, Heiberg, Og V. Kuhr, Einar W. Torsting,
and Niels Thulstrup. second ed. Copenhagen: Gyldendal, 1968-1978.

———. Philosophical Fragments. Translated by David Swenson. fourth
printing. Princeton, NJ: Princeton University Press, 1971.

———. The Point of View for My Work as An Author: A Report to History.
Translated by Walter Lowrie. New York, Evanston, and London: Harper & Row,
1962.

———. Training In Christianity. Translated by Walter Lowrie. reprint ed.
Princeton, NJ: Princeton University Press, 1971.

———. Works of Love. Translated by David Swenson and Lillian Marvin
Swenson. Princeton, HJ: Princeton University Press, 1946.

King, Martin Luther. A Testament of Hope: The Essential Writings of Martin
Luther King, Jr. Edited by James Washington. San Francisco: Harper & Row,
1986.

Klein, Stefan. The Science of Happiness: How Our Bodies Make Us Happy – and
What We Can Do to Get Happier. New York: Marlowe & Company, 2006.

Lasch, Christopher. The Culture of Narcissism: American Life in an Age of
Diminishing Expectations. New York: W. W. Norton & Co., 1979.

Luther, Martin. D. Martin Luthers Werke. Kritische Gesamtausbage. Weimar
Ausgabe. Weimar: Hermann Böhlaus Nachfolger, 1883.

Metz, Cade. "The Gender Gap in Computer Science Research Won't Close for
100 Years," The New York Times. June 21, 2019.

Murray, Charles. Coming Apart: The State of White America, 1960-2010. New York: Crown Forum. 2012.

Newberg, Andrew and J. Iversen. "the neural basis of the complex mental task of meditation: neurotransmitter and neurochemical considerations," Medical Hypotheses 61, no.2 no.22 (2003): 282-291.

———. and Mark Robert Waldman. How God Changes Your Brain. New York; Ballantine, 2010.

———. Why We Believe What We Believe. New York and London: Free Press, 2006.

Pérez-Alvarez, Eliseo. A Vexing Gadfly: The Late Kierkegaard on Economic Matters. Eugene, OR: Pickwick, 2009.

Pew Research Center. "U.S. Protestants Are Not Defined by Reformation-Era Controversies 500 Years Later," (2017).

———. "Where Americans Find Meaning in Life," https:www/pewforum.org/2018/11/20/where-americans-find-meaning-in-life [accessed April 20, 2020].

Phelps, Edmund. Paper presented at the Columbia Department of Religion and The Center on Capitalism, "Kierkegaard and Economics." 2013.

Reich, Robert. The Work of Nations. New York: Alfred A. Knopf. 1992.

Sapolsky, Robert. Behave: The Biology of Humans at Our Best and Worst. New York: Penguin, 2017.

Sennett, Richard. The Corrosion of character: The Personal Consequences of Word in the New Capitalism. New York and London: W. W. Norton & Company, 1998.

Stark, Werner. "Kierkegaard On Capitalism," The Sociological Review 42, no.1 (Jan. 1950): 87-114.

Sustainable Development Solutions Network. "World Happiness Report 2020," https://resources.unsdsn.org/world-happiness-report-2020.

Sweller, John. Instructional Design in Technical Areas. Camverwell, Australia: Australian Council for Educational research. 1999.

Twenge, Jean. iGen: Why Today's Super-Connected Kids Are Growing Up Less Rebellious, More Tolerant, Less Happy – and Completely Unprepared for Adulthood. New York and London: Simon & Schuster, 2017.

Walsh, Anthony. The science of Love: Understanding Love and Its Effects on Mind and Body. New York: Marlowe & Company, 2006.

Waters, Brent. Just Capitalism: A Christian Ethic of Economic Globalization. Louisville, KY: Westminster John Knox, 2016.

Wheeler, R.E., R. J. Davidson, and A. J. Tomarken. "Frontal Brain Assymetry and Emotional Reactivity: A Biological Substrate of Affective State," Psychophysiologie 30 (1993): 347-558.

Wolfe, Alan. Moral freedom: The Search for Virtue in a World of Choice. New York and London: W. W. Norton & Company. 2001.

Zak, Paul J. "Why Your Brain Loves Good Storytelling," Harvard Business Review" (October 28, 2014), https:hbr.org/2014/10/why-your-brain-loves-good-storytelling. [accessed April 24, 2020].

INDEX

A

absurd/paradox, 23-26, 51-54, 56-58, 65
Aesthetic Stage, xiii, xv, 19, 25, 28-38, 40-43, 45, 47, 52, 54, 57-58, 61-64
Amen, Daniel, 38n23, 48n9, 49n36, 60n12

B

Baby Boom Generation, 13, 34, 36
Barth, Karl, 68n10
boredom, xiii, 25, 31-34, 43, 56, 58, 65

C

Carr, Nicholas, 37n11, 38n12
careers, xii, 2, 4-5, 7-8, 12-15, 17, 18, 41-46, 62
Carter, Stephen, 59n5
Clinton, William, 12, 14
contemporaneity, with Jesus, 24, 54, 65-66
COVID, 57

D

Davidson, Richard, 17
death, 34-35
despair/anxiety, xiv, 7, 13, 16, 23, 34, 36, 45-47, 53, 55, 58, 61

E

Eberstadt, Nicholas, 48n16
Ethical Stage, xiii-xiv, xv, 25, 26, 39-49, 51-53, 56, 58, 62-64, 66
Existentialism, xiii, 21, 23, 25, 29, 52

F

Friedman, Thomas, xi, xvn1, 1, 2, 6, 7, 8nn1,4,9,15, 9nn18,22, 12, 19nn1,4, 42, 48n15
Friendship, vii, 18, 30

G

Globalization, xi-xii, xiv, xv, 2-14, 31, 36, 39-42, 45, 51, 53, 55-56, 58, 61, 64-66
Graeber, David, 19n11

H

happiness, xii-xiii, xv, 12, 23-24, 27, 31-32, 35, 37, 41, 46, 52-53, 55-56, 58
Hegel, G. W. F., 23

I

iGens, 5
internet, xi, 5-6, 13, 31, 33

K

King, Martin Luther, 68n10

L

Lasch, Christopher, 9n24
Leap, of Faith, xv, 37, 63
Luther, Martin, 17n13

M

marriage, 15, 18, 29, 30, 33, 42, 44
Millennial Generation, 4-5, 32, 36, 42

N

Narcissism, xii, 5, 7, 12, 14, 19, 34, 36
Neuroscience, xiii, xv, 5, 16-17, 31-35, 37n12, 41, 43-44, 46, 53, 54, 58, 65-66
Newberg, Andrew, 48n21, 60n12

P

Phelps, Edmund, 21, 27n1

R

Reich, Robert, 14
Religious Stage, xiv-xv, 47, 51-59, 63-67

S

Sennett, Richard, xvn2, 8n3, 9n23, 13, 19n6, 29n16, 39-40, 48n1,
sex, 30, 32, 37n12, 43, 46
subjectivity, 23, 25, 35-36, 40, 51-53, 59, 62

T

Team Management, xii, 2, 7, 15-16, 45
Trump, Donald, 12, 57
Twenge, Jean, 8nn16-17, 38nn14,31, 48n16

W

Walsh, Anthony, 20n20
Wolfe, Alan, 20n13

X

X-er Generation, 36

www.ingramcontent.com/pod-product-compliance
Lightning Source LLC
Chambersburg PA
CBHW070930270326
41927CB00011B/2799